THIS IS MY WAY

365 Positive Thoughts and Self-Care Journal

Daily Inspiration, Wisdom & Powerful Questions for Self-Reflection Diary

Mauricio Vasquez
Be.Bull Publishing

ISBN 978-1-990709-60-9

It's crazy how quickly an entire year can go by! With how busy we can get, it can seem like there is never any time to reflect on what has happened and how it has impacted us.

What if there was a way to find inspiration every single day? Not just here and there, but instead we would create a consistent, safe space for us to cultivate our confidence and build a better us!

This process is about more than one approach. Here are just a few benefits:

- Discovering what truly brings us joy and inspiration in life
- How journaling can be a powerful tool for our growth and self-guidance
- How positivity we can make our thoughts work for us and not against us
- That prioritizing our self-care will help create impactful, healthy habits

Every single day in our lives there are opportunities to grow or to remain where we are, but we can only choose the right one when we are prepared and ready for the chance itself! By developing a steady, one day at a time mindset that has been built on a foundation of self-care, confidence, and self-honesty, we will be able to make the best, healthy choices for our benefit whenever they come around!

Instead of taking this approach month-by-month, or even week-by-week, this journey is much more specific and focused on making sure that your growth is a daily occurrence!

Every day, there will be a unique, inspirational phrase to give us something personal and real to consider as we go about our day. Once we have dedicated time and thought to that inspiration, we will be met with a few questions as a guide to navigate us through the reflection process.

Whether we use that time to gain more control over our anxiety, building ourselves up through positive thought, or learning about how our actions impact the lives of others, not a day will pass when we won't discover something new about ourselves and also how we can improve on a consistent, progressive, daily basis!

This is more than self-help and more than just a book; this is a year that is about a deeper understanding of life, who we are, and what our purpose is! Let's discover the best version of ourselves and how to manifest that same improvement in all aspects of our lives. We are worth the 365-day investment and deserve the powerful results that will follow!

THANK YOU!

Thank you very much for giving me the opportunity to contribute something positive to your life. I hope this book will help you, and that you will enjoy what you can achieve after reading the positive affirmations and writing your responses to the powerful questions. I also hope that this book makes you reflect and that it fills you physically, psychologically, and spiritually. Thank you again!

Please, I want to ask you a small favor.

I do not have a large company, nor do I have a publishing company helping with the marketing and promotion of this book. I wrote and produced this book on my own. As a result, I will be very grateful if you can please give me a review on Amazon.

With your review, this book can improve (or worsen) its ranking on Amazon and become more visible to others, so that they can too benefit from it! **To give me your review on Amazon, please scan this QR code**.

Thank you very much in advance for your support!

Mauricio

Table of Contents

This book is dedicated to my family, my wife Devon, and our daughter Aria.

Thank you both for your support and love. You are both my rock and guiding light.

Love you, my girls.

Preface

I wrote this book to help me understand the process of self-improvement and to share that with you so we can go on this journey together. Although the book covers the 365 days of the year, that doesn't mean to say the journey lasts just one year. No, the first thing I learned on my journey was that it lasts as long as we want it to.

We can discover new possibilities through the positive affirmations laid out in this book and by asking powerful questions that challenge our minds and spirits. Questions that make us reflect and delve deeper into our consciousness. Questions like:

- How can we take responsibility for our lives?
- How can we bring more clarity to who we are and what is in our minds and souls?
- How can we transform ourselves for the better?

What could I bring to the table, though? What makes me so special to think I could help others? The truth is there's nothing special at all about me. However, the thing that I can offer is guidance. Having started on this journey, I can show you how I maneuvered around the obstacles, how I overcame the weaknesses and fear within me, and how we can now continue on this journey together.

This journey is a continuous battle to conquer the challenges that face us each day. We must welcome these challenges because they are what make us grow and develop as an individual. We all have a choice—allow these obstacles to block our advancement or advance through them on the path to self-improvement.

These tough experiences are unavoidable aspects of life, and so often, people feel alone and isolated in their situations. The goal for us all as imperfect humans is to rise above it and move forward!

It isn't about being rich, or famous, or any of those surface-level equivalents, because I am none of those. I'm just trying to set aside my ego and recognize that my humanity means that I am simply a work in progress. Where I was isn't where I had to stay, so I'm trying to improve myself. Not only that, but I learned anyone can improve themselves as long as they identify areas of improvement and then follow through on the actions needed.

With everything that is going on in the world, it continues to impress upon me how important it is to find daily worth and power in ourselves. So many people find that during bad times, the negatives seem to manifest themselves to a much higher degree; anxiety, feelings of isolation, job uncertainty, and a plethora of other concerns.

1

All these paths led me to where I am and where we are now, ready to create change, find positivity, and make every day an additional reason to be grateful.

Community is such an essential part of this journey, so if you want to connect with me, you can find me on LinkedIn. Please visit this link or scan the QR code:

linkedin.com/in/mauriciovasquez

All the best,

Mauricio Vasquez

Introduction

When was the last time you had a positive thought? I don't mean something in passing, but a time when you imparted wisdom to a deeper part of you? It has been far too long for many of us. When you think about it, this is what happens when we lift ourselves or give ourselves the affirmation we need. Positive thoughts encourage us to continue on the path we are on, or the confidence to change paths and take a new direction.

The good news is that science also backs up the benefit of those positive thoughts or daily moments where we take the time to give ourselves a boost. As incredible as our brains are, they still need a little help from time to time, and interestingly enough, one of those areas is our realization of self-worth.

Our minds can get a little confused about what is real and what isn't, creating a gap in reality. This may be a result of some negative feedback or a disagreement over something with a friend or family member. We may doubt our own viewpoint if we don't have the courage of our convictions, and their reality becomes ours.

When we put positivity into our day, it helps our brains grasp reality better. It helps us recognize our self-worth and see things with clarity, without all the junk that stops us from moving forward. That is what negativity is—junk that messes with our minds and holds us back.

That is more important to understand now than you may think, because many people have underlying or subconscious expectations and assumptions that manifest later on. Consider this your first test of being honest with yourself.

Is some part of you looking at this to improve an aspect of your life?

This is a pretty important question to ask. We all have our reasons for going on this journey, but unless we know the specific reason why we want to go through this process, we won't know how successful we've been at the end of it. We need something to measure our success by.

Using a journal has been proven to be an excellent way of collecting our thoughts and by responding to the questions in this book, we can examine our inner feelings. This method of self-reflection stems from the days of the Roman Empire, when Emperor Marcus Aurelius wrote a series of books made up of his own quotations. Despite experiencing war, plague, and an attempt to dethrone him by his closest allies, he found the time to put down his thoughts for his own self-improvement and guidance.

So often, we forget how powerful we are, just as ourselves! No matter how many times we hear that the ability to change lies within us, it just doesn't sink in. Well, that is because it takes time, patience, and a willingness to follow it through. Real, lasting change doesn't happen overnight, but with daily affirmations that uplift us and remind us of who we are, we can put that process into motion!

This is a "free form" experience, so whichever way *you* want to read this book is perfectly fine! As long as you are getting positive results, it is working.

You can take it day by day and go through it chronologically, so if you began the book on February 23, you would consider that your Day 1 and loop back around in a year. If you are someone who prefers not to go "by the book," then, by all means, find the places within this journey that speak to you and use them to inspire your life. The world is filled with more than enough stress and pressure; an experience meant to uplift and affirm shouldn't add to that negativity.

Each daily affirmation is set up to inspire and uplift with a quote that speaks to some aspect of our lives. Afterward, there will be questions to answer. This allows us to take a moment and not just read the quote, but let it sink in, and then the question can be almost like a mini-guided meditation. No need to worry; they aren't like the essay questions that were on school tests—these are gentle and meant to create peace within ourselves. The quote opens your mind up; the questions help you find where it fits for you.

Like the way in which you read this book, how you decide to answer the questions is entirely up to you! There will be space to write it all down here, but you are more than welcome to use a separate paper or type it out. If you are reading the Ebook, take a piece of paper to write your thoughts and responses to the questions. And if you are listing the Audiobook, you can pause the recording to think about the affirmations, questions, and responses, and if possible, you can also take a piece of paper to record whatever is on your mind. As long as you feel comfortable, you will gain more from this process when you take ownership and immerse yourself in reflection.

One of the most rewarding parts of this journey is when you read the quote, and like a spotlight, you see where that speaks to in your own life.

Making improvements to yourself is not meant to be swift; it is a gradual process that needs time to become lasting. A phrase heard often is to take life "one day at a time".Well, this experience is designed entirely around that idea—one day, one quote, one lesson at a time. You will be amazed at how that one quote and question can blossom into thought during the day and even lead you to some pretty amazing revelations about yourself.

Remember, obstacles can either block our way forward or we can advance through them in order to improve ourselves. That is your choice. It all starts with you and one day—everything grows from there.

This is your way!

Chapter One: January

    January is commonly the month where I can start afresh and look to the upcoming year, but the original meaning sheds some light on something often overlooked. The Roman god, *Janus*, is where this month's name is derived from. He had two faces; one that looked forward and another looking back. These features signified that while I should look to the future and prepare myself, it is just as important to look back and reflect on the road so far.

    While it is fine to make resolutions at the beginning of every year, maybe this time around, I focus on *myself* and use these upcoming months to inspire and better myself bit by bit. The journey is well worth the end, plus the growth along the way is inspiring.

    All that starts right here, and it can't begin without the first day...

JANUARY 1

I will trust myself to have the strength I need to take on risks and the upcoming challenges. Trust is about me having an optimistic and realistic belief in my true, inherent potential; both actualized and not yet actualized.

What are my realistic goals over this next year? Why are they important to me? What are the reasons behind my desire to achieve those goals?

_____

_____

_____

_____

_____

JANUARY 2

My journey is centered on learning as much as I can about my personal growth and development. Learning is where my progress begins; learning about myself and the world around me.

What is the one thing I can learn today that could help me to start with my personal growth and development? What would be the benefit of learning that?

_____

_____

_____

_____

_____

JANUARY 3

Every challenge I experience in life is a chance to be taught and an opportunity to grow and live with more purpose. My purpose is something bigger than myself—going beyond my needs—it is what will pull me into action. It is my compelling reason to be and do in this world.

What has been holding me back from living a more purposeful life in the past? How could I prevent this from happening again?

JANUARY 4

My strengths and gifts are my own; they will help me create a meaningful life. My strengths are the assets that I can tap into in times of difficulty. They are a source of my resilience.

What are some of those "strengths and gifts" that I rarely acknowledge in myself? What am I missing from not acknowledging and maybe even using them more in my life?

JANUARY 5

...ich I choose to start my morning can arm me to conquer the day ahead. How I start ...s how the rest of my day will go, taking me closer or further away from what I want to accomplish in the day.

What am I currently doing (or not doing) that might prevent me from setting my mind for success for my day? What's it costing me to continue to ignore the importance of my mornings?

_____

_____

_____

_____

_____

JANUARY 6

I will not allow other people's opinions of me to shape how I live my own life. My independence increases my self-value and self-esteem.

In the last year or so, what have I let someone else's opinion take away from me? How will I change this in the future?

_____

_____

_____

_____

_____

8

JANUARY 7

The goals I set today will end up forming who my future self is. Goals are how I translate my dreams into reality.

As of right now, what obstacles are in between a specific goal I have set and my current reality? What can I do to set my goal clearer and more reachable?

_____

_____

_____

_____

_____

JANUARY 8

Keeping a healthy mindset will help shape my understanding of both my possibilities and my limitations. A healthy mindset means that I am looking for solutions instead of focusing on my problems. A healthy mindset includes learning from my mistakes.

What could be negatively affecting my mindset? What can I do to improve the chances to identifying my possibilities and limitations?

_____

_____

_____

_____

_____

JANUARY 9

The more intentional I live my life according to my values, the more open I will be to having fulfillment and satisfaction. My personal values are a central part of who I am and who I want to be.

What are the most important values I show as the leader of my own life? What is the most radical step I can take to honor my values more fully?

JANUARY 10

Knowing myself means understanding my strengths individually and how they can work in connection with each other to continue my self-improvement. My strengths include my knowledge, attributes, skills, and talents that I can do well.

How deeply do I not only recognize but also own the strengths in my life? What are my top strengths I feel proud of? What do they bring to my life?

JANUARY 11

The more genuine I am with myself, the more authentic I can be in my expressions and how I relate to others.

What reasons would I have to not be comfortable with the genuine version of myself? What realistic changes can I make to my mindset right away?

_____

_____

_____

_____

_____

JANUARY 12

I will see the world as hopeful, even amid challenges. I will see the world as where I have a place of purpose and possibilities.

What do I currently understand about my purpose, and what do I still need to learn? What can I do to learn more about it?

_____

_____

_____

_____

_____

JANUARY 13

Even though it might not always be easy, I will let myself learn through trial and error. The most important life lessons I will ever learn will be from the poor decisions I make.

What successes and failures stand out to me in my life? What did I learn from them?

_____

_____

_____

_____

_____

JANUARY 14

An essential part of setting my goals is understanding my reality and what does and doesn't work best for me. I will set goals for myself, not goals for what others expect. My goals must be grounded in my purpose and vision.

What goals in my life are there simply because I think they should be? What is a new goal that I can set-up for myself in line with my purpose and vision?

_____

_____

_____

_____

_____

JANUARY 15

My life is not summed up by one moment or one experience. I am more than just what has happened to me, and I have control over my future.

What are the most significant gaps between where I am now and where I want to be in the future? What will I do to close this gap?

_____

_____

_____

_____

_____

JANUARY 16

All the change that I am purposefully manifesting starts with my awareness. My awareness is about the present state, and where I am right now.

What in my life needs to be let go of in order for me to move forward powerfully? How do I know what I am missing to see?

_____

_____

_____

_____

_____

JANUARY 17

I will find the courage to step outside of my comfort zone by understanding that it relies on my belief in myself. Stepping out of my comfort zone helps me live life at its fullest and mature and grow as an individual.

What was a situation where I stepped outside of my comfort zone? What did I win from taking this step?

_____

_____

_____

_____

JANUARY 18

As I make decisions in life, it creates a map that displays and reflects my values. This will help me learn more about myself, what matters to me, and what truly drives me.

What are the central values that help me navigate through life? How will those values help me find the way towards a goal I am pursuing?

_____

_____

_____

_____

JANUARY 19

I will not allow the "What Ifs" and "Yeah Buts" to constrain the powerful changes I decide to put into practice. Limiting beliefs are thoughts and opinions that I believe to be the truth, but have a negative impact by stopping me from moving forward.

What are the top three of those "What If" statements that are hindering my progress at work or home, or anywhere else? How will I address them the next time I face them?

_____

_____

_____

_____

_____

JANUARY 20

Having a realistic view of my capabilities is what will start creating an optimistic trust in myself and what I can do. My capabilities are skills and abilities that I do well and that I bring to the table as a person, student, or professional.

What are some of my skills or abilities that I do not let out of the box? Why do I hold these back from both myself and the world? What can I do to use them more?

_____

_____

_____

_____

_____

JANUARY 21

It is far better for me to listen more and ask better questions. Questions breathe life into knowledge, and both of these enrich my life. When I do all these things, I shall be better and more diverse for it.

Where in life have I wanted to know more about something but let how I felt or how others thought hold me back from fulfilling my curiosity? What could I have done differently to avoid others from impacting my learning?

_____

_____

_____

_____

_____

JANUARY 22

It is vital to have relationships built on collaboration. My life is made on the contributions of many, not just my own. When I fully accept this, I will discover new aspects of myself I didn't realize before.

Who are the people in my life who can both challenge me and push me to grow? Do I feel like I genuinely appreciate them? What can I do to express more of my appreciation to them?

_____

_____

_____

_____

_____

JANUARY 23

My life's experience comprises both enjoyment and fulfillment. The things I do and learn about, what I love to do, are where my enjoyment is. The quality of the person I am becoming and what I bring to the world; that is my fulfillment.

Am I balanced in how I view enjoyment and fulfillment? Which do I lean towards? Why is that?

_____

_____

_____

_____

_____

JANUARY 24

Whatever I achieve or do not accomplish in this life is my responsibility. I will hold myself accountable and celebrate when I win, and learn when I lose. There is no room for denial.

When was a time in my life when I didn't take responsibility, one way or the other, that had a significant impact? How did I learn from this?

_____

_____

_____

_____

_____

JANUARY 25

I will not let the things that happen around me control what happens in my own life. My environment does not get to define, control, or create who I am. I take ownership of everything in my domain, including the outcome and everything that affects it.

Are there things or points of negativity that I am still allowing in my life even though they only hinder me? What are some of those, and what can I do to have more ownership over them?

_____

_____

_____

_____

_____

JANUARY 26

I have the power within me. I will learn how to access that power to become more intentional, be more committed, and inspire myself to action!

When was the last time I found inspiration in myself? What steps can I take to bring out this power more often?

_____

_____

_____

_____

_____

JANUARY 27

When I challenge myself, I will not do it simply for the sake of it. I will be purposeful and use my capabilities to fuel my response to the challenges.

Have I been challenging myself incorrectly? Where can I adjust so that I still grow from being challenged but do so in a targeted, direct way?

_____

_____

_____

_____

_____

JANUARY 28

A purposeful life is a choice I can and will make each day. I will make it my energy source, directional compass, and how I shape my life. A purposeful life is when I am moving towards a big goal in my life that aligns with my values, passions and makes me happy.

When I really think about it, do I begin my day in a way that sets me up for success? What are a few specific ways that I do not set myself up for success? What can I do to improve those areas and focus on using the morning as a springboard for the day?

_____

_____

_____

_____

_____

The best way to achieve the dreams and goals I have is to remain committed to my beliefs and the actions I choose to take. I will reach what I set out to accomplish by holding myself to what I commit myself to do every day.

If I had to summarize the core beliefs in my life, what would they be? What are one or two beliefs that I haven't remained committed to that I should have? How can I repair that?

_____

_____

_____

_____

_____

January 30

The world is filled with more than enough limitations. I will not place them on myself; instead, I choose to see my full potential realized for myself and for my loved ones. My limitations are not objective breaking points; they are just what I choose to believe to be the limit.

When I read the word "limitation," what in my life comes to mind? How can I improve and move past that?

_____

_____

_____

_____

_____

JANUARY 31

Life is made up of choices, from when I wake up to when I fall asleep. I will strive to make the best decisions for my growth and use those choices to become the version of myself I am aiming for. Every decision count to move me forward or backwards.

Thinking about a specific situation in my life where I am not achieving the results I'd like, if I am being honest, are the choices I have been making progressing or hindering my growth? What would be the reason for that, and how can I make those changes?

_____

_____

_____

_____

_____

Every month there will be a time meant for looking back over the inspirations I found, progress, or areas that need change. In this space, I can jot down notes on my thoughts, summarize the month, or specify the impacts that came from my daily moments with myself.

As always, it is my absolute best that I am aiming for, and times to reflect can be where we find the most inspiration.

Monthly Reflections

What did this last month mean to me?

_____

_____

_____

_____

What daily inspiration had the most meaning to me?

_____

_____

_____

_____

This month I learned…

_____

_____

_____

_____

22

Chapter Two: February

February gets a bad rap for being sort of a "let-down month" because of all the attention that January gets with resolutions and the New Year. Some people even misspell it and get frustrated, not to mention that it's the shortest month. All that can make it challenging to continue any momentum from January. There must be a better way to enjoy a month as fantastic as February can be.

Let's do away with the old attitude and go into this next month with a positive mindset and a belief that February can be even better than the one before. There is the chance to reflect and have the opportunity to both remember and see where I want to be as I improve. It's a month of Valentine's, Julius Caesar, and the elusive Leap Year day.

Carry the mindset of possibility and new perspectives going forward so that each month is a chance to become better than I was.

FEBRUARY 1

I will keep my mindset of living purposefully by remembering that life will happen for me, not simply to me. The first one takes me in a direction of deeper growth, learning and healing. The second one leads me down a path of victimhood and martyrdom.

What recent situation could I have made happen *for me*, and why didn't I take action? What steps can I take so that next time I will consider a problem or issue as happening *for me*, and not *to me*?

_____

_____

_____

_____

_____

FEBRUARY 2

Choice is the cornerstone of what makes me alive. In my humanity is the freedom and responsibility that comes with that kind of choice. I will endeavor each day to fully appreciate that. Choice is not just about choosing among the existing options; it is also about creating new ones.

When was the last time I let a choice be influenced by something other than my accountability and responsibility? What was the outcome, and how would I act now?

_____

_____

_____

_____

_____

FEBRUARY 3

Life isn't just about me; there is a world filled with valid and different perspectives. Being able to appreciate that and grow by exploring other views is an important part of my process. I can remain true to my core beliefs and still learn from how others see life.

If I am being honest, do I keep my mind open enough to learn from others? What steps can I take to improve this and start opening up more to the experience and wisdom of others?

_____

_____

_____

_____

_____

FEBRUARY 4

My learning is not anyone else's responsibility. In order for me to grow, I must take advantage of the opportunities to learn, while maintaining my integrity and being authentic. Learning will allow me to adapt, to survive and thrive in this new era.

What is something that I can open myself to in the coming weeks? What about in a more long-term way of thinking? What could be the benefit of learning that?

_____

_____

_____

_____

_____

FEBRUARY 5

Accountability is one of the most important characteristics of change. Being accountable bridges the gap between my intentions and the actions I end up taking. Without it, I will not grow to my full potential.

Where is an area in my life where I need to be more accountable? What actions can I start to take today that will begin that process?

_____

_____

_____

_____

FEBRUARY 6

I will not allow my situation to define the choices I end up making. Instead, I will take initiative and action to create my own path with decisions based on what is best for me and my future.

Both at work and at home, what is an example of a time when my situation dictated how I reacted? Have I changed that since then? If not, how can I initiate that self-improvement?

_____

_____

_____

_____

FEBRUARY 7

The closer I get to understanding my purpose and my mission on this earth, the more complete my life shall be. My purpose is my path that provides orientation. I will strive to learn and evolve so that each experience I have can be as fulfilling as possible.

As of right now, what do I believe my purpose is? In the coming weeks, what can I do to get closer to understanding what I am meant to do?

_____

_____

_____

_____

_____

FEBRUARY 8

Where I place my attention in life is where the most growth and progress occur. In my work, at home, and with my relationships, I will strive for balance so that my growth is spread out and my life flourishes.

Is there one area of my life that gets more attention than the others? Why is that? Are there steps I can take to start balancing that out? What are they and how can I begin that?

_____

_____

_____

_____

_____

FEBRUARY 9

Curiosity does not have to be a negative aspect of my character. I can use my curiosity to drive my attention, my desire to explore, the risks I am willing to take, and the knowledge I open myself up to. I will learn how to use my experiences to continue feeding my curiosity, and from that feeding my process and growth.

Do I view my curiosity as a positive or negative? What can I do to make good use of my curiosity and let it work for me?

_____

_____

_____

_____

_____

FEBRUARY 10

My awareness of both myself and the world around me is key in shaping both who I am and who I will become. Using my awareness, I can expand my experiences, take more effective actions in my life, and trust that my path is leading me in the right direction.

Am I open toward the world, or is my awareness more focused on my individual experience? What can I do to expand that so I can grow in a more balanced way?

_____

_____

_____

_____

_____

FEBRUARY 11

The experiences of those around me are not only valid, but they are excellent resources to learn about the perspectives of others. I will continue to learn from their advice, expertise, and backgrounds rather than viewing it as an obstacle in my own experience. Learning from other people's mistakes and successes is an efficient way for me to figure things out on my own.

Not counting those in my intimate social circle, who in my life has been the most influential? Who currently holds that position and why do they fill the role?

_____

_____

_____

_____

_____

FEBRUARY 12

I set my pace, the world does not set it for me. I will make time for reflection so that what I learn can be fully embraced and absorbed. I will not be made to feel guilty about prioritizing my growth and health over an expected pace of life.

Where in my life could I slow down, even a bit? Are there actions I can take to start easing up a little, and if so, how do I begin to take them?

_____

_____

_____

_____

_____

FEBRUARY 13

My life isn't just about choosing what is already there, it is about setting new goals, blazing trails, and new experiences. What makes my life spectacular isn't what I am doing, but who I am while I am doing it. The person I am becoming will create options for myself, and not simply accept what exists.

When I look at my life, are my choices created by me, or were they because they were just there? What steps can I take to become more aware of the kinds of choices I make?

_____

_____

_____

_____

_____

FEBRUARY 14

Love is not an obstacle, nor does it hold me back. I am the person I am because of the love I have received, and because of that, I can now do the same for others. Life is not just about knowledge and experience, it is about love as well; for others, for myself, and for the journey.

In my life, is there a balance of love between myself and others? What can I do to either love myself more or show others that I love and care for them?

_____

_____

_____

_____

_____

FEBRUARY 15

My attitude can help or hurt my situation. I cannot expect to flourish if my attitude doesn't match. From now on I will pay more attention to my mindset and how it is setting me up for either success or struggle. By taking responsibility for these outcomes, I will gain more control in my life.

What was a difficult situation where I had the wrong attitude and didn't succeed in what I wanted to achieve? What could have been the reasons for my wrong attitude? How can I prevent this from happening again in the future?

_____

_____

_____

_____

_____

FEBRUARY 16

Part of understanding who I am as a person is being truthful about the strengths and gifts I have. By uplifting myself and viewing my characteristics through a positive lens, I will learn how to appreciate all parts of the person I am, and who I am becoming.

What are 3-5 strengths or gifts of mine that I rarely let out of the box? Why do I hide these, and what can I do to utilize them more often to help my growth?

_____

_____

_____

_____

_____

FEBRUARY 17

My strengths in life don't grow and become stronger on their own. It is my responsibility to not only recognize my strengths, but to hone them, value them, and learn all I can about them. The more knowledge I have about my strengths, the better I can use them throughout this journey.

Which strength of mine do I rarely work on? Why do I have that approach? What will I start doing so that I enhance that strength, and then others?

_____

_____

_____

_____

FEBRUARY 18

My purpose is not what I do, but who I am being. Understanding my purpose and meaning in life is not a singular moment, it is an ongoing conversation. Every day I add more to the dialogue, but it is never fully finished. I need to be dynamic and purposeful in my actions.

Do I ever address my meaning and purpose? Why or why not? How can I incorporate that into my life so that I stay focused on what I am aiming for?

_____

_____

_____

_____

_____

FEBRUARY 19

Self-care deserves to be a priority in my life. My wellbeing will rely on being balanced in my mental, physical, and emotional state. Unless I recognize the importance of addressing each aspect, I am not truly balanced.

How do I care for myself? Do I feel like I prioritize my self-care? If not, why and how can that be changed? What would it cost me if I don't do anything about it?

_____

_____

_____

_____

_____

FEBRUARY 20

The actions I put forth in my life deserve excellence. I will let myself be guided by my desire to be committed to bringing excellence to everything I do. Every day is a chance to put my best into the world. Doing your best means never stop trying.

As I am right now, what role does excellence play in my life? Do I strive for it, or do I consider it to be something unattainable? What will help me change my attitude and thus my relationship with excellence?

_____

_____

_____

_____

_____

FEBRUARY 21

I will learn to trust my intuition and do so through the rule of three: be open to what I feel, speak it into existence, and trust it to come into being. I am capable of building this trust with myself.

Do I trust my own intuition? What is standing in the way of that intuition becoming a tool instead of a fear? How would I diminish its power so I can better trust my instincts?

_____

_____

_____

_____

_____

FEBRUARY 22

The positivity I can bring to the world is not contained to one part of my life. I will commit to creating change on a positive level through the conversations and relationships I have.

Where does positivity play a large role in my life and in my relationships with others? Where do I want it to be manifested more than it currently is?

_____

_____

_____

_____

_____

FEBRUARY 23

I recognize that my life affects more than just me. The influence I have must be both wholesome and positive. It starts with me and ripples outward, but it is my responsibility to be aware of how I utilize my influence.

Where in my life do I hold influence? If I am honest, do I use that influence to the best of my ability and for positive, productive reasons? How will I commit to improving that going forward?

_____

_____

_____

_____

_____

FEBRUARY 24

My assumptions are there to be questioned for me to have a greater grasp on reality. I will not let those assumptions become my mindset, instead, I will be objective and methodical in testing my assumptions to find out their truthfulness.

What are some assumptions in my life, past and present, that do not line up with the core beliefs and values I am building? What am I doing, or what will I do, to continue working on the assumptions that remain?

_____

_____

_____

_____

_____

FEBRUARY 25

I am creating change every single day. I am doing this through my ambition, my drive to be better, the ability to self-start, and how I am capable of taking charge. These characteristics are my tools that will build what I am working towards.

Other than the four characteristics above, what parts of me would I consider go-to tools in my "toolbox"? How have these worked in my favor in the last months?

_____

_____

_____

_____

FEBRUARY 26

My positivity and optimism will enable me to make the most out of whatever situation I find myself in. By being consistent in both those characteristics, I am setting myself up to succeed and make positive impacts. My optimism can protect me against sadness and anxiety.

In the last year, when did my "positivity and optimism" make a challenging situation into one that was easier to handle? Adversely, when did I miss a chance to use those characteristics and how can I not miss out next time around?

_____

_____

_____

_____

FEBRUARY 27

When I give myself the time and freedom to reflect on the things I have learned, I open myself to new depths of learning. When I do reflect, I will do so without judgment and start the work on what I discover about myself without negativity.

Do I let myself reflect enough, honestly? Knowing my schedule, when can I make even a little more time for these reflections? What could be the downside of doing that?

_____

_____

_____

_____

_____

FEBRUARY 28

When I discover new things about myself that need to be worked on I will use the situation to my advantage. Each of those moments is an opportunity to consider my choices, where I currently am, and what I can do differently.

What characteristic of mine am I too hard on myself about? Am I doing enough work on that part of myself? If not, what steps can I take to change that?

_____

_____

_____

_____

_____

FEBRUARY 29 (Leap Year)

When I acknowledge the pace I need to be at, despite what the world says, I will use this for my benefit. Slowing down or taking a break is important in recovering from my work and responsibilities. This will fuel my progress and become the reasons my dreams come true.

Considering that this day is rare, what is something about my progress or self that I do not give enough attention to? What will I do so that when the next Leap Year comes around I have made changes in this area?

_____

_____

_____

_____

_____

Monthly Reflections

What did this last month mean to me?

_____

_____

_____

_____

What daily inspiration had the most meaning to me?

_____

_____

_____

_____

_____

This month I learned...

_____

_____

_____

_____

Chapter Three: March

This entire journey through daily inspiration is all about refreshing and renewing myself. In the spirit of that, did I know that March was the beginning of a new year for quite some time—even as late as the 1750s? Instead of just letting that be another historical fact, I'll use it as another chance to have a beginning. January, and sometimes December, tends to be where I could go for reflection, but that is a change that can be made here and now.

How many times have I reached the month of March and felt some significance? It's important to not let any of these moments become usual or commonplace. The world might not give March its due, but for a month named after the Roman god of war, I would think a little more respect would be in order.

So, in this period where Spring begins and I have a brand-new beginning all over again, build from there. Each day, take in the inspiration and remember that a fresh start can come at any time.

MARCH 1

Being self-aware means knowing about both the good and the bad. I will use my awareness to enhance my strengths and work on my weaknesses. I am not weaker by acknowledging where I need to focus more attention.

What are two of my strengths and two weaknesses? How do I use my strengths? What am I doing to improve my weaknesses?

_____

_____

_____

_____

_____

MARCH 2

My purpose is not just about me. True satisfaction is found when my purpose encompasses both myself and one that is beyond me alone. Purpose is related to how I will show up and BE with those people around me.

In this year so far how have I used my purpose, or journey towards my purpose, to better others instead of myself? What is standing in the way of doing it more often?

_____

_____

_____

_____

_____

MARCH 3

I am learning to let go of my need to look good when it is to my detriment. I will also work towards not needing to always be right. My need for both these things gets in the way of the journey I am on.

Which of those is more important to me; being right, or looking good? What is the reason behind that? How can I start making progress towards changing that?

_____

_____

_____

_____

_____

MARCH 4

The gifts and strengths that are within me are unique to my experience. If I focus on developing my strengths, I can grow faster than when trying to improve my weaknesses. I will go into each day committed to using them to create a meaningful life.

What would be gained from committing myself to showing more strengths at work or home? What can I do so that tomorrow does start that way?

_____

_____

_____

_____

_____

MARCH 5

My purpose is bigger than what I can imagine. It is not contained to a strategy or goal; it is a living, changing entity. Seeking my purpose will draw meaningful goals and strategies to me, but neither defines what my purpose is. I will treat it like what it is; fundamental to my existence.

What do I decide to be my purpose moving forward? What would the search for my purpose bring me? What is at stake if I don't find my purpose?

_____

_____

_____

_____

_____

MARCH 6

I will be more aware of how I treat and respond to my emotions. They are not my enemy, nor are they a detriment to my journey. I will learn how to understand my emotions and use them as positive information along the way. My emotions help me to know what I need and want (or don't want).

Do I see my emotions as positive or negative? How has that perspective impacted my life thus far? Do I need to make changes there? If so, what changes and how can I begin making them?

_____

_____

_____

_____

_____

MARCH 7

I will focus on what is happening to me now. My present is where I can bring about change. I will learn from my past, and work towards my future—but I will live in the present.

Would I say that I tend to live in the past, present, or future? Why do I live this way? How can I bring about more balance and attention to the present?

_____

_____

_____

_____

MARCH 8

There is no such thing as a moment in which there is nothing I can do. Even though I might not be able to take action or change the situation, I can help myself and others during it. Just because I can't do what I would like to, doesn't mean I can't make the situation better.

When there is a situation in which I feel like I can't do anything, how does it make me feel? Does it end up causing me to try and fix it even though I know I can't? How can I make changes to this pattern?

_____

_____

_____

_____

MARCH 9

I can't control everything. There will be times when things happen, and I will have no control over them and I accept this. Even though I may not be able to control it, I can control my reaction to the situation. That is power in itself, and I will work on recognizing that.

When was a recent time when I had no control but reacted well? What about when I didn't react well? What was the difference between the two, and how can I make the positive reaction the norm?

_____

_____

_____

_____

_____

MARCH 10

I will not assume that I am doing everything right. By taking the time to check, I will make sure that my attention is where it should be. It is my responsibility to ensure that my focus is on essential parts of my life that are within my control. I will not waste any more energy on things I cannot change or control.

What triggers cause my focus to drift? Am I doing enough self-checks, or any at all? What more can I do to keep my attention where it needs to be?

_____

_____

_____

_____

_____

MARCH 11

I take my responsibilities seriously. In everything I do, I strive to bring my absolute best. My resourcefulness and authenticity are tools I can use to my advantage. When I allow my best parts to work together, I can create real change.

Would I say that I really try to bring my best all the time? Where am I easing up on the gas? Can I change something about that, and if so, what?

_____

_____

_____

_____

_____

MARCH 12

Self-care matters in my life. When I am not at my best, I run the risk of not bringing everything I have. My state of being and well-being affect my mindset and abilities. I will do better at recognizing when self-care needs to be made more of a priority in my life.

What is my preferred form of self-care? Do I think I prioritize myself enough? Where is an area in my life that isn't at its best because I didn't take care of myself? How can I get better with that?

_____

_____

_____

_____

_____

MARCH 13

My goals, whether they are big or small, rely on my motivation to make them a reality. I will use my small goals as building blocks to manifest my bigger goals. I will keep small goals simple and achievable so that I can feel the momentum of small wins.

Off the top of my head, what are two or three small goals of mine? Two or three big goals? How do they work with each other, or how can I help them to build off each other?

_____

_____

_____

_____

_____

MARCH 14

My goals are there to help me advance my life and purpose. They are not there to give me a reason to break myself down. If I do not complete a goal, I am not a failure. I do not measure myself based on the number of goals I set and reach. I measure my success based on the person I was and who I am now. If I improve, then I succeed.

Do I place too much weight in accomplishing goals? How can I shift the focus back to the big picture instead of on the small things in between?

_____

_____

_____

_____

_____

MARCH 15

In order to grow as a person, I must learn to set aside what I think I know and replace it with what I actually do know. Holding on to old ways of thinking will only keep me from the new knowledge I am aiming for.

When I need to make a decision, how would I know if my opinion doesn't reflect reality? How could I identify and avoid my unconscious biases?

_____

_____

_____

_____

_____

MARCH 16

I can start working towards increasing the wisdom in my life at any time I desire. The foundation for this is created when I have more questions and fewer answers. Sometimes my questions are more important than the answers.

What role does curiosity play in my life? Is it beneficial to my growth or is it a hindrance? What can I do to create positive curiosity?

_____

_____

_____

_____

_____

MARCH 17

Where I am right now is not a place of completion. I am a work in progress, and that is something I do not judge myself for. I will continue to adapt and evolve as my life progresses, but I am never a finished product.

How does it make me feel acknowledging that life is a process and not a goal? Is my current attitude in this hurting or helping me? If it is hurting me, what can I do to change it?

_____

_____

_____

_____

_____

MARCH 18

While it is important to listen to productive self-criticism, I will not let my inner critic control me. I will be aware of the difference between advice and judgment, especially when it comes to me. I won't allow myself to be the judge, jury, and executioner.

What was a situation where I was very harsh with myself? How strong of a pull did my inner critic have at that moment? What will I do to lessen the weight it carries at the next opportunity?

_____

_____

_____

_____

_____

MARCH 19

When I am clear in my commitments and responsibilities, it goes a long way toward helping me be guided by my purpose. I understand that intentional living will shape the direction of my life. My intentional living is about creating healthy boundaries.

Regarding my "purpose", what responsibilities and commitments are helping me towards my goals? What kind of boundaries can I set around them to protect them from external forces?

_____

_____

_____

_____

MARCH 20

My strengths can be fuel for my responsibilities. When I learn to combine the two and let them work for each other, I will be contributing to my overall well-being. I will focus on doing the right things and doing things right.

What are my strengths that could be used to help me in my responsibilities? What can I do so that in the future I recognize this more naturally?

_____

_____

_____

_____

MARCH 21

I will not have goals just for the sake of having them. Creating meaningful goals that are fulfilled through intentional living will lead to satisfaction in knowing I make progress. With having meaningful goals, I am more likely to stay motivated and accomplish my objectives.

Are there goals in my life that are just "there"? Can these be adjusted to become more meaningful, or do I need to remove some? Which ones, if any, do not meet my criteria any longer? What would be the reason for that?

_____

_____

_____

_____

_____

MARCH 22

Many things are positives in my life and help me grow; fear and anxiety are not in that category. Neither contribute to productive learning and will only weigh me down. I will not be constricted by negative characteristics, instead choosing a better focus for my attention.

What roles do fear and anxiety play in my life? Am I letting them in under the guise of "tough love"? How can I fight them off in the future?

_____

_____

_____

_____

_____

MARCH 23

My awareness is one of the key tools to finding and understanding my purpose. By recognizing that, utilizing reflection and self-inquiry, I will be more prepared for a journey of excellence, and deeper meaning in my work and life.

If I am being honest, how much work am I putting into being aware? What is stopping me from giving it more effort and focus?

MARCH 24

I have the freedom to choose, but I also must recognize the responsibility that comes with that. My choice may be mine, but that does not mean that there won't be results from that choice—positive or negative. The more I understand this, the wiser my choices will become.

When I make my choices, do I usually know what the results will be? How often do I do it anyway, regardless of the consequence? What will I do to improve the quality of my choices, and what assists them?

MARCH 25

In a chaotic world, my principles are what can ground me in reality and my journey. By understanding those truths, I can lead a more wholesome and effective life. My principles are my moral rules or beliefs that help me know what is right and wrong, and that influence my actions.

What are three of my main principles that guide my choices? Recently, how has each contributed to my well-being? How can I better honor my principles?

MARCH 26

I recognize the power of attention to detail. By taking greater care to notice the usually missed details in my life, I can find a greater and deeper understanding of my reality. My reality is the sum of noticed and unnoticed details.

How would I rate my attention to detail regarding the issues I face? Could there be things that I could improve about it? If I am not already doing those, why not and how will I start?

MARCH 27

I understand that every situation might not be able to be fixed, but I also recognize that each situation is workable. When I take the time to consider the possible solutions, I will be able to work on the problem instead of assuming it can't be fixed.

Do I truly carry the positivity of that quote into the difficult moments of my life? If not, why don't I? Is this something I'd like to change, and if so what are the first steps?

_____

_____

_____

_____

MARCH 28

Every day, I will strive to create a world where there is freedom and safety for each person. I will not only do this through my actions but also through my mentality and attitude—even amid difficulty.

This year, how have I worked towards creating that kind of world? What can I do in the next months to continue or initiate a positive momentum?

_____

_____

_____

_____

MARCH 29

I understand that in life, there will be challenges. I am willing to take risks and make difficult choices in order to overcome those challenges. Even when it isn't easy, I will strive to be victorious in those times of hardship.

When was the last time I had to make a really tough choice in order to bring a positive result to a situation? What did I learn about myself? What can I do to continue being able to make tough decisions?

_____

_____

_____

_____

_____

MARCH 30

Life isn't just about one view. When I can see things from multiple perspectives, I will be able to bring wisdom to the issues and problems I encounter. My wisdom is best viewed from the multiple perspectives I can access.

What can I be doing to ensure I see things from more viewpoints than just my own? How can I inspire myself with a commitment to shift my viewpoints and find new possibilities for reflection and action?

_____

_____

_____

_____

_____

Good things in life do not just happen. In order for me to obtain consistent positive and productive results in my life, I must do three things well; prepare, execute, and follow through. When I commit to all these steps, I will be setting myself up for continued success.

Of those three phases—prepare, execute, follow through—which is my strength, and which do I need to work on more? How can I improve on my weaker points here?

_____

_____

_____

_____

_____

Monthly Reflections

What did this last month mean to me?

_____

_____

_____

_____

What daily inspiration had the most meaning to me?

_____

_____

_____

_____

This month I learned...

_____

_____

_____

_____

Chapter Four: April

This month is like opening a box filled with all different kinds of snacks and trinkets because there is so much happening! You have a day dedicated to pranks, one dedicated to trees, there is of course, Easter, and a day celebrating Earth itself. Quite ambitious to pack so much into one month, but April gets it done and does it in style!

With so much going on, it might seem difficult to find a theme, but with every special day and event, there is one overarching ideal that shines through; *love*. You can start with the month being named after Aphrodite, who is known for being love manifested. Spring brings with it the sense of refreshment and renewal, but also new love that is "in the air" throughout the month. Throw in that the birthstone is a diamond, and you can see how April is the month that puts love right out in front.

Let's use every day as a new chance to learn more about love, and how it can be shown to ourselves and others!

APRIL 1

I understand the potential for my actions to either progress or hinder my journey. When I live with an attitude of awareness, my actions will not only set me up for success, they will display my true intentions.

In my day-to-day life, how can I be more aware of the impact my actions have? This last week, in what way have I set myself up for success through my actions? What about ways that have not done that?

_____

_____

_____

_____

_____

APRIL 2

Being flexible, especially in moments of difficulty, will enable me to thrive regardless of what is going on around me. I can function in a wide variety of contexts and situations. The more I can adapt, the more I will rise above.

Would I consider myself a flexible person? How does this help or hurt my progress in life? What changes can I make right away to help me become a more flexible person?

_____

_____

_____

_____

_____

APRIL 3

I allow my values and principles to dictate my actions, rather than allow outside influences to do so. When my beliefs and ethics are in line with reality and truth, I can trust them to send me in the right direction. Finding consistency in choosing my principles is one of the most important lessons I can learn.

How often do I let other people influence the actions I take? Why is this? What steps will I take, both now and long-term, to shift my attention inward?

_____

_____

_____

_____

APRIL 4

Living a full life means understanding that the learning never stops. I will put in the effort to ensure that my desire to learn never diminishes, but also to find ways that will improve how I learn. Being devoted to my self-education shows faith in myself.

f I am being honest, am I open to learning new things about myself and life? What could be holding me back from wanting to continue that learning portion? How can I set out to learn one new thing a month about my journey towards achieving the goals I have set and having the kind of life I desire?

_____

_____

_____

_____

APRIL 5

Opportunities in life will not be handed to me, so I will open my eyes to see each chance that life brings to me. I understand that when I open my eyes and identify those opportunities, my growth will exponentially increase as well. The first step I can take towards having a brighter life must be to increase the awareness I have of my surroundings.

When was the last time that I recognized an opportunity that others did not? What characteristic of mine enabled me to do this? What can I do, or am I doing, to continue that trend?

_____

_____

_____

_____

_____

APRIL 6

The tasks I set for myself and the ones that work towards my self-improvement are necessary, important, and deserve my attention. I will strive to build my discipline so that I can stay on task and continue my personal growth.

Do I have a system in place to help me complete the tasks I need to—schedules, journal, planner, etc.? How can I improve the methods in which I go about addressing the things I must do in my life?

_____

_____

_____

_____

_____

APRIL 7

Every experience in my life is a new chance to learn and grow. I will revel and take joy in the positive, but also gain understanding and perspective from the negative results. When everything is a learning opportunity, I can overcome anything. In a life of valleys and mountains, there is value in seeing value all around.

Do I tend to lean more to extremes when it comes to the results in my life; do I get too happy about the wins, and too down about the losses? How can I bring balance to my life in these regards?

APRIL 8

My life is about balance. I will find safety and refreshment in my comfort zone, but I will not live my life in that place. I will push myself, take risks, and learn to grow. When I can exist in both the comfort zone and the places that challenge me then I will find true personal growth.

Being honest with myself, do I spend too much time in my comfort zone or could I learn to expand my horizons more? How can I bring more balance to that? What is creating that imbalance in the first place?

APRIL 9

To progress in life, I do not have to know everything about everything. I recognize the value in not having all the answers, and being able to grow in life despite that. I will not allow my curiosity to become a hindrance. Being able to accept the unknown is a valuable lesson for me to learn.

Do I let my curiosity derail my progress? If so, why does the need to know mean that much to me? In the present, how can I accept what I do not know?

_____

_____

_____

_____

_____

APRIL 10

I will challenge the assumptions in my life and use different perspectives to nurture new ideas. When I do not rely on what I think I know, and instead discover what is real, I can find previously unseen possibilities. Living outside of my own opinion is a healthy practice to adopt. This means finding value in what other people think and seeking to understand why they have those opinions.

Is it hard for me to change an assumption I have? If so, why is it more important for me to be right than for the truth to be right? What will I do to challenge those assumptions?

_____

_____

_____

_____

_____

APRIL 11

Acknowledging reality will go a long way toward creating a true perspective of my life. I will recognize what I have done, come to terms with what I have not done, and work to learn and be aware of what the future can be. I do not benefit from staying in a vacuum of my thoughts.

Of those three phases (what I have done, what I have not done, and what the future can be) which do I have trouble with and which am I most comfortable with? Am I okay with this dynamic, and if not, what will I do to change it?

APRIL 12

I understand that learning is not always an easy process. I must be willing to be challenged and stretched past where I am comfortable to learn certain aspects of life. By accepting and recognizing this truth, I am more prepared for when those lessons arrive.

What are some of the more challenging lessons I have learned? Do my feelings on how that occurred impact my preparation for future lessons positively or negatively? How can I improve my attitude regarding this?

APRIL 13

I recognize that because of the need for balance I must find value in both optimism and seeing reality. I do not need to choose one or the other. By crafting my perspective around both of these views I can have a well-rounded, strong approach to life.

Am I an optimist, a realist, or a pessimist? What am I doing to remove the pessimism and focus on the other two? What steps can I start taking to create a balance between just optimism and realism?

_____

_____

_____

_____

_____

APRIL 14

I will not get bogged down by frustration amid a situation. Instead, I will become agile and able to adapt as the circumstances shift around me. When I can adjust to the demands, even as they change, I will be able to avoid unnecessary stress and grow from each experience.

When the demands of a situation change, do I react correctly? Why or why not? What can I do so that the next time things shift, I respond productively?

_____

_____

_____

_____

_____

APRIL 15

I am not powerless over my habits. The ability to change and improve is completely within my control. My awareness and strength will help me know which choices are right for me.

What are some habits of mine that I have wanted to change, but have not yet? Why haven't I made those changes? What is my plan to start making those changes a reality in my life?

APRIL 16

The relationships in my life are a gift. Even when challenging times come, I will not forget that the people I love and those who love me are what matter.

Even in the closest relationships, there can be struggles; where in my life is there a relationship that needs attention? In the next month, what actions can I take to improve this relationship?

APRIL 17

What I can accomplish and the belief I have in myself are interconnected. Whatever challenges or difficulties come my way, if I truly believe in my ability to conquer it, then I shall. There is power in believing in myself.

In the last month when did my belief in myself work in my favor? What about when it was not a strong point? How will I start to make positive changes in my self-worth and value in my own eyes?

_____

_____

_____

_____

_____

APRIL 18

Finding success in my work is all about balance. Being able to invest myself in my profession means understanding the importance of investing in my personal life as well. Taking care of myself will only work for my benefit in all aspects of my life—profession included.

If I could make three changes in my work situation, what would they be? What is standing in the way of me making those changes in real life? What impact can I make in the next month? 6 months? Long-term?

_____

_____

_____

_____

APRIL 19

I am worth my own attention and focus. By including self-care in my routine, I prove to myself that it matters. Every time I prioritize my well being I bring increased balance to my life, which improves it overall.

In the last week, how have I taken steps to bring attention to my self-care? What about the opposite; when, if I have, did I set my well-being aside? In each situation, why did I react as I did? What does this tell me about how I view my self-care?

_____

_____

_____

_____

_____

APRIL 20

The little things in life are sometimes the most memorable. Just because something isn't considered "productive" doesn't mean it doesn't add richness to my life. Enjoyments like hobbies are not only beneficial, they give me a glimpse into different perspectives.

Do I have areas of my life that could be considered "for fun" or a hobby? If not, why isn't that a part of my schedule? How can I help myself see these "fun" activities as a positive addition to my life?

_____

_____

_____

_____

_____

APRIL 21

Because my time is valuable, the way in which I use it really does matter. Whether it is too much work or too much play, having control over where my time goes means having control over the balance of my own life. Having opportunities to manage my time is a blessing and will benefit me in the long and short term.

What does the term "time management" mean to me? In what ways can I improve my relationship with this practice—even if I already consider it a strength? What are two ways in the next weeks that I can make real, tangible improvements to my time management?

_____

_____

_____

_____

APRIL 22

I will learn the different ways to love those around me, and myself. The way I express love towards those in my life has meaning, so I will put effort into loving people as individuals and not simply in general.

What are some different ways I express my love to others without saying "I love you"? Not just in romantic relationships, but in the other ones in my life, do I express love comfortably? What can I do to start making that a more natural act?

_____

_____

_____

_____

APRIL 23

Being happy is just as important a part of my life as any other pursuit. Feeling joy is something that I not only deserve but also strive to incorporate into my daily situations. When I only look for the negative, that is what manifests, so I shall seek the positive and my happiness.

Where, in comparison to other parts of my life, do I prioritize my happiness? In what ways have I put other things before my joy, and how have those situations impacted me—positively or negatively? How can I turn those negatives into positives?

_____

_____

_____

_____

APRIL 24

Life is filled with chances to be brave in the face of difficulties. I have courage and bravery inside me, even if I feel fear in situations. Just because I am afraid or trepidatious about something doesn't mean I can't be brave—there isn't courage without fear.

Would I consider myself a "brave person"? Why or why not? How can I remind myself that bravery exists in the midst of being afraid, and not be disheartened?

_____

_____

_____

_____

APRIL 25

Just because something didn't happen when I wanted it to, doesn't mean it isn't going to happen. My timing isn't the standard, and the more I recognize that the more energy I can save. Being attentive, focused, and motivated means more than needing something to happen right away—if it means I have to wait.

When life doesn't go by my timing, how do I usually respond? Is that response something I would consider productive and in my best interest? If not, what can I do to change my reaction so that I don't impede my progress through impatience?

_____

_____

_____

_____

_____

APRIL 26

Balance isn't just about work and personal life, it also means putting weight in my dreams and goals. Even if something feels far off and out of reach, by believing that my dream is worthwhile and attainable I will achieve it one day. All that can only happen when I allow myself the freedom to dream in the first place.

Both in a long-term and short-term sense, what are 3 dreams that I currently have or have had in my life? In the next 6 months, what can I do to make strides towards at least one of these goals?

_____

_____

_____

_____

_____

APRIL 27

In the pace and hustle of life, I cannot forget that taking care of my physical self is just as important as my emotional self-care. The more I treat my body with respect and positive attention, the more I show myself that I am a person of value. The way I treat myself—inside and outside—matters in the way I view myself.

Everyone says they want to take better care of themselves, but do I give attention to my health like I should? Why or why not? How can I make my health a priority for me, not just now but for the future as well?

_____

_____

_____

_____

_____

APRIL 28

My words matter, but my actions will reflect who I truly am. I recognize that the habits I choose to keep and those to change will contribute to the person I end up becoming—and who I am right now.

What are 3 habits that have made positive contributions to my life? How do I keep those habits strong? What lesson from my positive habits can I apply to the negative ones?

_____

_____

_____

_____

_____

APRIL 29

I am not in this life alone; the people I choose to love and surround myself with have an influence on me. By seeing value in myself I will set out to also remove the negative influences that have been impacting me.

Do I do enough to make those positive influences in my life feel appreciated? How can I do more to show them that their impact matters to me? What steps can I take to make sure that in the future I can be more expressive with my appreciation?

APRIL 30

When I let doubt cloud my expectations of myself and life I am not setting myself up for success. The more belief I let in, the more doubt will be removed, making room for progress, productivity, and success. Beginning from a place of belief makes all the difference.

Do I begin most of my endeavors from a place of belief in myself, skepticism, or doubt? Why do I start out with this state of mind? How will I bring about change to this aspect of my life so that I am accomplishing what I set out to do?

Monthly Reflections

What did this last month mean to me?

_____

_____

_____

_____

_____

What daily inspiration had the most meaning to me?

_____

_____

_____

_____

This month I learned...

_____

_____

_____

_____

Chapter Five: May

Since the days of the early Roman Calendar, the month of May has been known for renewal and fresh beginnings. The snow has thawed, animals are waking up from hibernation, and the first day of Spring cannot wait to shine once again. Do you know what the best thing about May is? That it can mean so many wonderful things for each of us—that means you as well.

What places in your life need reexamining? Are there emotional spring cleanings that should be taking place? How about dreams and goals that you have yet to tackle? When it comes to refreshing ourselves and the theme of *renewal* it doesn't have to be confined to one thing or one area of your life. So, in the spirit of beginnings and taking on new things, move forward ready to learn about yourself and where your life is going.

MAY 1

Living a positive, fulfilling life means understanding that the learning process never ends. The more open I am to accepting life lessons—new or adjusting my thinking on the old—the better my life will become overall. I will strive to avoid stagnating, instead of pushing to always learn more.

How do I rate myself from 1 to 10 in terms of my openness toward new learnings? How can I keep myself open to learning new lessons, especially coming from others? If I'm being a bit defensive in those situations, what steps can I take to be more receptive and open to what I might need to learn?

_____

_____

_____

_____

_____

MAY 2

I will recognize the place that creativity has in life. It isn't just about art or creating things, it is about finding those little, special places in life that matter to me. By recognizing the importance of being creative and growing that part of myself, I will be honing balanced well-being both now and in the future.

In what ways do I feel comfortable expressing myself creatively? If I do not feel comfortable, how can I start to make changes to my outlook on that matter? What can I do now so that in the future I see the importance of creativity?

_____

_____

_____

_____

_____

MAY 3

The way I view time matters. If I am constantly negative and stressed about how much time there is—or how little time—then I am not creating an environment for positive growth. However, if I approach time with patience and a positive attitude I can create a more healthy relationship with how I manage time.

Do I see time through a positive or negative lens? Why do I have this perspective? Whether my relationship with time is good or bad, how can I begin to improve it going forward?

_____

_____

_____

_____

_____

MAY 4

Self-control is very important in life, but I also need to be aware of where it should be applied. There is a difference between self-control and not wanting to take a risk for the sake of protecting myself. By strengthening my awareness I am also making sure that I know what is too much of a good thing, and when I should try something new and bold.

What role does self-control play in my life? Have there been instances where I haven't taken a step forward and justified it as self-control? How can I work towards being aware of the difference?

_____

_____

_____

_____

_____

77

MAY 5

Love is not meant to be confined to just one area of my life. I can cultivate love in my home, within my profession, in my friendships, and in the activities I enjoy experiencing. I will work towards being more open and letting love into all the aspects of my life. Love makes me stronger.

What places in my life, if any, am I not comfortable letting love into? Why do I feel like I need this separation? How can I take down these walls I have put up against love in those areas? What would be the value of doing that?

_____

_____

_____

_____

MAY 6

Just as it is important to find purpose in my work, it is just as vital for me to find those places where I can seek my happiness on a different level. Whether it is a hobby or some other enjoyment, there is nothing selfish about wanting to experience these places of happiness by myself. I will remember to make room for those happy areas in my life.

What can I do to make happiness a priority in my life? What relationship do I currently have with experiencing happiness? How can I improve that relationship?

_____

_____

_____

_____

Succeeding in life isn't just about having a positive attitude, it is also about being brave enough to push through everything in the way. I will not let fear stop me from achieving what I have set out to do, and my courage will help me navigate those challenges.

When life becomes challenging, how do I usually respond to the past? What is one situation in which I was brave despite what was going on? How can I learn from this for my future reactions?

_____

_____

_____

_____

_____

MAY 8

I believe that the goals I have are worth working towards. I know that there will be times when I will want to rush, but in those moments, I will remember that patience calms the chaos. When I can bring a patient attitude to my daily life, I will be setting myself up for continued success.

What are some triggers in my life that make me want to rush? In those moments, why is patience difficult for me? How will I bring positive changes to that process?

_____

_____

_____

_____

_____

MAY 9

There is room for both reality and my dreams to exist together. I can aim for the sky and dream big, but also be grounded and pragmatic. With belief in myself and awareness of my strengths and weaknesses, I can be real while not lessening my dreams.

What are 2 goals I consider realistic and 2 goals I think are more like dreams? What can I do to work towards both of those at the same time and not lose focus on either?

_____

_____

_____

_____

MAY 10

My mental health is not something for me to hide or apologize for. I will remember that I do not have to adjust who I am for anyone else, and that includes my mental health. When I can prioritize myself instead of what others think, I am truly on the path to living a healthy life.

What parts of my mental health have I covered up or apologized for in the past? What can I do in the future so that I respond in a healthy way that puts my well-being first?

_____

_____

_____

_____

MAY 11

When I choose to overlook negative habits instead of confronting them, I am seeing my future self as a priority. While it might be easier to let those things slide, when I take responsibility and bring improvement to those areas I am saying that my personal growth is worth it.

What are a few bad habits of mine that I tend to overlook because it is easier to not see them? On a personal level, why do I let those slide? What can I do to improve those bad habits and to choose my personal growth over the easy choice in the future?

_____

_____

_____

_____

_____

MAY 12

The best way for me to grow as a person is to surround myself with people who can teach me. Even though it may be easier to interact with people who do not challenge me, I must not miss out on the chance for growth simply because it takes less effort. The relationships in my life have an impact on me, and because I can control who is in my life I can decide whether that impact is positive or not, and whether I am being open to learning new lessons or not.

Why have I chosen the relationships that impact me the most? Have those been positive or negative impacts? What steps can I take so that those relationships I choose in the future are for positive growth reasons?

_____

_____

_____

_____

_____

81

MAY 13

Belief, regarding the people I surround myself with, can be a circular thing. It is important for me to believe in myself, but for those I love it is just as important for me to believe in them. Understanding this will help me remember that I am not alone, and that where I place my belief matters. For when I believe in others, those I love will also believe in me.

Is it easy or hard for me to accept that others believe in me? To believe in me? Whether it was easy or hard, why do I feel these ways about others and myself?

_____

_____

_____

_____

MAY 14

There is nothing wrong with being deeply invested in a multitude of hobbies, just as there isn't anything wrong with being fully dedicated to my profession. The important key to that balance is recognizing when action is needed to correct that balance. When I can honestly confront those corrections and follow through rather than ignore them, I will have a better grasp of what true balance in life is.

In regards to my profession, what issues have I had with balance in life? Have these issues been more about personal or work imbalance? As I stand now, what do I need to do to either create or continue balance across my life?

_____

_____

_____

_____

MAY 15

There isn't room in my life for both proper self-care and guilt over taking the time for it. When I make the time to rest and give attention to my physical and emotional self, it is so I can press on afterward. Guilt will just negate the rest I am striving for, so by removing it and accepting self-care as a priority in my life I am choosing a healthy future for me and my loved ones.

In regards to the time needed for self-care, what role has guilt played in those decisions? What can I do to eliminate guilt from having a say in the matter? What steps will help me remember to keep self-care as a priority?

_____

_____

_____

_____

_____

MAY 16

I will start to see creativity as a valuable asset of my life. When I make room for my creativity, I am putting worth in how I express myself. This will expand my emotional IQ and pave the way for further creative growth. My creativity is a source for increasing confidence in my potential.

What are some mediums through which I feel comfortable expressing myself creatively? If I have trouble with this, why is that? And what steps can I take to incorporate more creativity in my regular routine?

_____

_____

_____

_____

_____

MAY 17

My priorities are a window into what I value in life. Understanding this will allow me to invest my attention and resources into what really matters to me. When I am more aware of this process, I can see if there are areas of my life in which I need to readdress some priorities.

If I am being honest, even sometimes do I put my priorities on autopilot? What can I do to bring more attention to the things I prioritize? How can I make this a consistent focus?

_____

_____

_____

_____

_____

MAY 18

It is important for me to understand that my perspective does not negate how others feel; I may think they understand how I feel about them, but that is not the reality. Understanding that, I will begin paying more attention to whether I tell others what they mean to me or if I continue assuming they know. By recognizing the difference between knowing I love someone and actually telling them I love them, I am willing to see from their point of view and not just my own.

Would I consider my comfort level with the emotional expression a strength or weakness of mine? What can I do, or what am I currently doing, to help develop more comfortability with that?

_____

_____

_____

_____

_____

MAY 19

Finding things in life that I enjoy and seeking happiness are lifelong endeavors. By keeping myself aware and open to new interests and joys, I will begin discovering happiness and learning lessons in places that I hadn't seen before.

In the last few months, what are several new interests or hobbies that have become a part of my life? How am I keeping myself open to these new joys in the future? If I am not, what can I do to start the process of being open?

_____

_____

_____

_____

_____

MAY 20

Courage is an aspect of my character with a diverse number of applications in my life. The more I recognize that, the more areas of my life I am willing to be courageous in. Courage is needed to love, to change, to try new things, to make hard choices; understanding this will strengthen all parts of myself.

What is an area of my life that I show or have shown courage in? What areas do I feel I could be more courageous in? What are the things I could do to boost my courage?

_____

_____

_____

_____

_____

MAY 21

There are people in my life who see me in a leadership role, so the example I set matters. By understanding how I am seen and the influence I have I can learn more about myself and the kind of leader I am and want to be.

What are some of my characteristics that help the kind of leader I am? What about the qualities that do not help? How could I enhance those qualities? How would I describe my leadership style?

MAY 22

The more I want to rush the process of things in my life, the less I will be able to learn from the journey. Patience isn't just about being willing to wait, it means putting in the work so that when I reach my goal, I am prepared to fully embrace, understand, and enjoy it.

What are the main reasons why I tend to rush things? How can I start to slow down and appreciate the process? What would be the specific value of that on my life?

86

MAY 23

The important part about having dreams is that I do not lose hope when things don't go the way I expected. However, it is normal if that happens. While it is vital to have goals, dreams allow me to believe that I am capable of more than just the logical and possible.

What is a dream that I am currently working towards? What is helping me keep believing in that dream? How can I apply this to other dreams or goals in my life?

_____

_____

_____

_____

_____

MAY 24

Integrity means that I hold myself to the same ethics when I am in private as I do when I am in public. Consistency across all those aspects of my life creates a healthy balance. Achieving consistency is about loving not only the targeted results, but also the process.

Where are the areas in my life where I am not as consistent as I would like? What would be the reasons for this? How can I be more consistent and find that balance?

_____

_____

_____

_____

_____

MAY 25

It is more important for me to be honest with myself about what I need to adjust in my life rather than avoiding difficult changes. The more transparency I have with myself, the more I set myself up for positive and productive changes.

What areas of my life do I tend to sugarcoat to avoid the difficulty? How can I prioritize honesty in those areas? What is the immediate first step I can take?

_____

_____

_____

_____

_____

MAY 26

Even though sometimes the work ahead of me seems insurmountable, I am capable of succeeding. By taking these situations one step, one moment, and one action at a time, I am building habits that will help me in the future. Step by step I will be able to improve my confidence and results.

What is a specific area in my life right now where the workload is a point of stress? What steps can I take now that I haven't taken in the past to help me succeed this time?

_____

_____

_____

_____

_____

MAY 27

The depth of the relationships that I have are parallel to the investment I have in them. The people I choose to give my time and attention to will be the relationships that are the closest and most important to me. By seeing my time as valuable, I will be more discerning with my close relationships. Not all relationships are meant to last.

Which relationships in my life do I need to devote more attention to? Why have I not been doing so? How will I start adjusting in that particular relationship, and in my important relationships overall?

_____

_____

_____

_____

_____

MAY 28

Belief is an important part of life. Whether it is my belief in myself, something bigger than me, the people in my life, or simply belief in positivity, it matters. By allowing myself the freedom to believe, I put my strengths into my purpose.

What things in my life would I say I believe in? Where does belief have a difficult role? How can I keep being open to believing in the future as well?

_____

_____

_____

_____

_____

MAY 29

The skills, ability, expertise, and work ethic I bring to my profession are valuable; and their combination makes me unique. There is nothing wrong with wanting a healthy work environment where those traits of mine are recognized and appreciated. I deserve to feel needed.

In the past, when was there a work-related instance where I made my value a priority, for example, when I needed to defend my work and contribution? How can I use that to inspire the same in the future?

_____

_____

_____

_____

_____

May 30

Being aware of my self-care means doing what is necessary for my overall health, not only what I want to do. I will be committed to being attentive to all the ways I need to care for my well-being. The more I invest in this balance, the more natural it will become.

What are 2 aspects of my self-care that I do not enjoy? Focusing on those, what can I start doing right away to not avoid them in the future? What will be the benefits of improving on them?

_____

_____

_____

_____

_____

MAY 31

I can combat the areas of frustration in my life with a willingness to learn. When I stop giving my focus to the problem and begin investing it in learning how to handle the situation, I will find solutions. The lower the frustration in my life, the more open my vision is to opportunities to grow.

Recently, when did I choose to learn over being frustrated? What usually makes me focus on the frustration? What are a few ways I can set myself up for success in this area?

<u>Monthly Reflections</u>

What did this last month mean to me?

_____

_____

_____

_____

_____

What daily inspiration had the most meaning to me?

_____

_____

_____

_____

_____

This month I learned...

_____

_____

_____

_____

Chapter Six: June

June is unique in that it was once half of a large, more seasonal period of time known as Liao. The change in weather that signaled the end of Spring brought with it hotter temperatures. Liao meant *calm*, considering most time was kept by the sun and the days got longer, the daily work could be spread out over more daylight hours and thus it had the potential to be less stressful than usual.

In that spirit, this month can be seen as a time to start bringing about change. Lean into the *Liao* feeling and enjoy the calm, creating it when you can't find it.

JUNE 1

Just because something might not be considered significant to others does not mean I need to lessen its value to me. This applies to my feelings, but also in the ways I choose to enjoy myself. My enjoyment is a worthwhile part of my self-care without the addition of outside opinions.

What are some past enjoyments that I let what others think get in the way? Since then, how have I made positive growth in that area? What current hobbies fill that role of enjoyable activities now?

JUNE 2

The more value I place on my time, the more I will pay attention to what I invest that time in. By being aware of the areas that do not deserve the time they are getting, I can bring a more positive balance to my schedule overall.

Being honest, what are at least 2 areas that are currently getting more of my time than they should? What is the cost of investing my time in things that do not deserve it instead of being focused on what is worthwhile? How can I correct that?

JUNE 3

Success can be an important part of my life without taking away from my appreciation of the journey. Being able to love the process of life, and not only its destinations, will help me in the future by giving me a more enhanced appreciation of the goal itself. Success is not only about the result, it's mostly about the journey.

In the past, has taking the time to appreciate life been a priority for me? What is different about how I am now? What are a few ways I can begin incorporating this appreciation more?

_____

_____

_____

_____

_____

JUNE 4

Life is full of decisions and my happiness deserves to be considered when making those decisions. Sacrifice is needed at times, but it is not necessary for me to completely ignore the impact that my choices will have on my happiness. Being happy shouldn't be a deciding factor, but it should be in the conversation.

Do I tend to take my happiness into account when making decisions? How has this perspective impacted me; positively or negatively? Going forward, what can I do to be better in this area?

_____

_____

_____

_____

_____

JUNE 5

It isn't always easy to make difficult decisions, but it does take courage to do so. I will start giving myself more credit when I show bravery in the face of life's challenges, instead of simply expecting myself to. Self-affirmation and appreciation will help create a strong foundation that will build my confidence and self-worth.

In the last month, what was a difficult decision I had to make? How was I courageous instead of not making any choice? What can I learn from that experience for my future?

_____

_____

_____

_____

JUNE 6

The people who I consider role models should be in that position for a reason. I will be cognizant of the impact others' influence might have on me, including those I see as leaders. My respect is to be earned, and that includes those people who have authority roles in my life.

Am I discerning when it comes to the people I see as leaders in my life? Why or why not? How can I use caution and experience when selecting these figures in the future?

_____

_____

_____

_____

JUNE 7

The best things in life are found when I am willing to be patient and let it happen in its own time. There is wisdom in patience, and the more comfortable I become with that characteristic, the more I will appreciate what I gain in life.

Simple question; am I a patient person? What would help me strengthen my patience? What is one particular trigger for rushing that I can begin working on right away?

_____

_____

_____

_____

JUNE 8

Being realistic is important, but so is having something larger than life to reach for. Having a dream to pursue brings an added sense of inspiration and purpose to my life. I will never let my life become one without a dream in it.

What would a few of the more interesting items be on my Bucket List? What am I doing to keep the pursuit of them alive? What am I gaining from letting myself have a dream that is worthwhile?

_____

_____

_____

_____

JUNE 9

Even though it can be difficult and conflicting at times, I recognize that honesty is one of the more vital characteristics that can be gained in life. I will make honesty a consistent priority, even when it makes a situation uncomfortable. Truth is worth more than my comfort in the long run.

In the past, why have I chosen to avoid honesty to also avoid a conflict? How can I learn from those experiences? What will help me keep honesty as a priority even when it isn't easy?

JUNE 10

Just like there is no balance when I ignore my mental health, the same happens when I let my physical health slide. When I put effort into my own well-being and health, I am telling myself—and my insecurities—that I have worth in both mind and body. A healthy mind in a healthy body is what makes me complete.

What role does my physical health play in my priorities? What is preventing me from taking a more active stance for it? What are 2 ways I can start improving my physical health?

JUNE 11

I am learning to take responsibility in my life, and that includes understanding what I do or don't do and the reasons for my actions or inactions contribute to my positive or negative habits. When I realize the importance of taking responsibility, I will see the need to put thought into each choice I make, regardless of how significant I consider it.

What are some areas in my life where I let my habits slide a bit? Has this negatively impacted me, and if so, how? In the future, how can I come at this from a more productive perspective?

_____

_____

_____

_____

_____

JUNE 12

Life is not meant to be spent avoiding interactions or assistance from others. While there can be positives in doing something on my own, there is nothing gained in not accepting help from those in my life. Allowing myself to be a part of a community will help me succeed, not weaken me because I need others. And others need me.

How do I feel about allowing others to help me? Why do I, or have I, felt like I needed to do something without any help? How can I improve in that aspect?

_____

_____

_____

_____

_____

JUNE 13

There is great joy and benefit found in having the support of others, but at the end of the day, the most important thing is that I believe in myself. By building a foundation based on a belief that I can succeed, future conflicts and challenges will not take away that belief.

What is, or has been, the biggest reason I have trouble believing in myself? What have I done, or what will I do to build that faith in myself?

_____

_____

_____

_____

JUNE 14

There is nothing wrong with me having ambition. I am allowed to want better for myself and my loved ones and put in the work needed to get there, all free from outside negative influences and judgments. With focus, determination, and ambition on my side, I am giving myself the best chance to succeed consistently.

When was the time I buried my ambition? Why did I do this? Alternatively, when did I follow that ambition? How can I use these experiences to build a better foundation for the future?

_____

_____

_____

_____

JUNE 15

An important part of my self-care is identifying areas in my life that are sources of negativity. When I am real about what those areas are, I can change them, even if it is difficult and may create conflict. Without first removing the negative, I cannot fully increase the positive.

What are 2 areas of negativity that I have trouble dealing with? What has stopped me from removing them so far? What will allow me to follow through?

_____

_____

_____

_____

_____

JUNE 16

It isn't enough for me to just learn things that need to be changed I have to take action. Awareness is the first step, and I am committed to not just identifying but also doing what is needed for my present self improvement and for my future self.

What parts of my life do I see need work, but have yet to act? Why am I holding back? What are a few ways I could take action in these areas?

_____

_____

_____

_____

_____

JUNE 17

Being empathetic is an admirable trait, but I need to recognize the difficulties as well. True empathy means seeing things as another would, and even though that isn't always easy, I will use that characteristic to improve. I can become a better friend, partner, and person if I am willing to see what empathy wants to show me.

What are some reasons that I have not been empathetic in the past? What can I do so that empathy is a priority in my perspective? How can I enhance my empathy?

_____

_____

_____

_____

JUNE 18

When it comes to my creativity, I will learn when my expectations are needed and when they are not. There is value in creativity without a goal other than enjoyment and finding peace. The more I understand this, the more I can get from my creative moments.

Generally, by what criteria do I judge my own creativity? How can I ease back and find a way to be fulfilled by it without needing expectations?

_____

_____

_____

_____

JUNE 19

The more I see time as a guideline and not an absolute, the less stress I will have when managing it. Even though I know it isn't easy, when I can live more flexibly, I will have a clearer picture of how my time should be divided.

When I think about time, what reaction do I normally have? What about the impact time management has on my well-being? How can I take a healthier approach to planning my time in the future?

_____

_____

_____

_____

_____

JUNE 20

When I wait and hope for inspiration to come, I am not setting myself up for success. However, when I work towards the drive and put effort into myself during the process, I will not only be able to seek success but also know how to handle it when I reach it.

How do I get inspired? How can I use what drives me to prepare for the work it takes to succeed?

_____

_____

_____

_____

_____

JUNE 21

I am a unique individual, and because of that, I receive love in my own way. It is my responsibility, though, to be aware of my preferred method and see enough worth in myself to express it. By understanding this in myself, I can aim to love others as they prefer as well.

Not necessarily a "love language", but what way do I prefer to receive love? Is there a manner in which I show love as well? How can I use the information I learn from the two prior perspectives to better love myself and others in the future?

JUNE 22

In life, the happiness I bring to myself is just as important as the happiness I can bring to others. When I limit myself in any capacity, one way or the other, I am also limiting the ability I have to enjoy life, and appreciate the joy in others.

Which means more to me, my happiness or the happiness of others? Why do I feel this way? What steps do I need to take that will bring more balance to my views on happiness?

JUNE 23

It takes a courageous heart to take on a challenge, but it takes one braver still to pick myself up after a failed attempt and try again. As long as I get back up, I will never truly fail.

What is a common reason that "getting back up" has been difficult in the past? Is it still an issue for me? What will help me rebound easier in the future?

_____

_____

_____

_____

_____

JUNE 24

Success is built on both a grasp of reality and the ability to imagine. When I see less value in my imagination regarding my success, I am limiting myself. To truly achieve what I set out to, it will take reality and imagination together.

Am I more reality-based or imaginative? Why? What can I do to become a better combination of them both?

_____

_____

_____

_____

_____

JUNE 25

In my life, it is vital for the areas where I invest my loyalty to have worth and substance. As long as I remain aware and diligent, loyalty is a wonderful attribute for me to grow. I am also working to be aware of the difference between loyalty and obligation and act accordingly.

What am I loyal to in my life? Is there anything, present or past, that does not deserve my loyalty? How can I rectify that?

_____

_____

_____

_____

_____

JUNE 26

I am the leader of my destiny. And being a leader does not only mean one thing, it requires a wide array of characteristics. To be the best leader I can be, I need compassion, patience, and a willingness to learn about the things I do not know yet.

When I am in a leadership role how do I react when I need to adapt or adjust? What do I need to do to be more flexible while still being a good leader?

_____

_____

_____

_____

_____

JUNE 27

The more of a desire I have to speed up a process, the more I need to strengthen not only my resolve but also my patience. When something is truly worth having, it is worth the time it takes me to get there. I will remind myself when things get difficult that those characteristics come into play the most when I need to be steadfast.

How do I usually react when I get impatient with a process? What is one way I can do better in the future? What about in the more immediate term?

_____

_____

_____

_____

_____

JUNE 28

When I keep myself open to new experiences and new perspectives, I am giving my worldview a chance to grow. An open mind is the best way for me to experience all of the world instead of resigning myself to an isolated view.

What are 2 ways I consider myself open-minded? How about 2 areas I need to improve in being open? How could I boost my open-minded perspective on the world and on people?

_____

_____

_____

_____

_____

JUNE 29

A key part of my success is remaining humble, no matter what happens. It is easy to get caught up in succeeding, but I recognize how important it is to act in a spirit of humility. It is possible to be proud of myself without it becoming a negative trait.

How does humility play a role in my life? What are some things I can do to be more aware of whether I am acting in humility or not?

_____

_____

_____

_____

JUNE 30

The different things I want to achieve are valuable, and worth taking the time to see whether they can happen. Simply because something seems out of reach or challenging does not mean it is not worth the effort to pursue.

What is something I want to pursue but have been holding back? What has been stopping me up to now? What is one thing I can do to deal with what has been holding me back?

_____

_____

_____

_____

Monthly Reflections

What did this last month mean to me?

_____

_____

_____

_____

What daily inspiration had the most meaning to me?

_____

_____

_____

_____

This month I learned…

_____

_____

_____

_____

Chapter Seven: July

     July got its name from one of the more ambitious figures in history, despite the tragic ending; Julius Caesar. It wasn't just because of his power or political influence, although that is a common understanding. Julio Caesar was actually the one who made some changes to the calendar created by the Romans, which led to the same one we are still using. Somehow, despite that impressive contribution to modern record keeping, most remember Caesar for something else entirely. What do you want to be remembered for?

     This month is a good time to remind ourselves that everyone has a place in history, whether it is creating a calendar that lasts for 2,000 years or something else entirely, as long as it is personal and meaningful, your legacy can be whatever you want to make it.

JULY 1

I have a choice between being honest about what will help me achieve my goals and wanting something else to help instead. The right path to actually finding success doesn't always have to go the way I want to get me there. I will have faith that if I am honest with myself, I will reach my goals.

What is one honest thing that will help me get closer to one of my goals, but that I have not implemented yet? Why haven't I? How can I put that into practice as soon as possible?

_____

_____

_____

_____

_____

JULY 2

My health is about much more than just me. It is about taking care of myself to be there for those I love. It is about setting a good example for those who look up to me. It is about showing myself daily that I matter. By making my health a priority, I can do all this and more.

Of the reasons above, which is the best motivator for me to prioritize my health? What are 2 reasons that were not stated earlier that help?

_____

_____

_____

_____

_____

JULY 3

It is important for me to see repetition as building a solid foundation for a future habit. At my work, at home, or socially; reminding myself of this will help me avoid seeing it as mundane and view it as a positive, productive path. A path that will take me to my happy place.

What have I found to be the most effective way for me to form a habit? Which positive habit of mine can I use as an example for this process? Why that habit?

_____

_____

_____

_____

_____

JULY 4

When I see each interaction I have throughout the day as a new chance to positively affect someone, I will have a firm grasp on true compassion. It takes nothing away from me to be kind to someone else, so I will strive to see things through that lens.

When I react negatively to an interaction, what is the usual reason? What changes can I make so that I affect the interaction positively and not choose a negative response?

_____

_____

_____

_____

_____

JULY 5

I will work to bring organization into my life without being frustrated by the process. The more organized my life can be—in a way that is productive for me—the easier I can move forward feeling confident I am headed in the right direction. The effort is worth the result. I am capable of putting in the effort even when it is challenging.

What would I consider to be the most disorganized part of my life? Why is it that way? What steps can I take to make organization a regular part of my routine to deal with the disorganized areas of my life, but without adding unneeded stress or frustration?

_____

_____

_____

_____

_____

JULY 6

There is nothing wrong with evaluating my work situation when I feel it is needed. When I get uncomfortable examining where I am I need to recognize the signal that a change might be needed. When I am aware of how I honestly feel about my profession and its impact on me, the more I can make positive choices for my future.

Do I give myself the freedom to truly examine my work situation? Why or why not? How do I feel about my work situation? How can I improve it?

_____

_____

_____

_____

_____

JULY 7

The way I react to my self-care is signaling one of two things to me. Either I prioritize myself and am willing to make time for self-care, or I see other things as more worthwhile and put my self-care lower on the list. The more I lean one way or the other, the more I strengthen that view. It is my responsibility to make self-care something important in my life.

Regularly, what signals do I give about my self-care? What is the reason that I see my self-care the way I do? In what area of my life do I need to take better care of myself? What is a specific way in which I can practice this kind of self-care and how does it benefit me?

_____

_____

_____

_____

_____

JULY 8

When life's challenges knock me down, I have the option of seeing it as a disappointment or a chance to gain more experience. In life, I learn when I am willing to see mistakes as something necessary and, in the long run, positive. When I am open to falling a few times, I will set my fear aside and choose to learn instead.

How do I usually view the times in life I didn't succeed? What are a few lessons, if any, that I learned from those times? What steps can I take now so that I am open to mistakes in the future?

_____

_____

_____

_____

_____

JULY 9

The more I am able to see from someone else's perspective, the more overall understanding I will gain of myself. Empathy teaches compassion, and from that, I will be able to forgive, relate to, and love myself and others more. I am worth that effort.

What is one way that empathy has taught me something about myself? What about a time I didn't empathize? How did I—or how can I—learn from that as well? What could have I learned from such an experience?

_____

_____

_____

_____

_____

JULY 10

Whether I realize it or not, the ways I choose to divide my time end up telling me where to direct my energy and focus. This thought might not be in line with my true self and the values I hold. Outside of my obligations, I have choices as to where my time goes, and those areas are where my focus and attention should be as well. By understanding the importance of where I place that attention, I will be discerning about the investment of energy it has the potential to be.

When did a lack of balanced time management harm my life? What did I learn from that? With better time management, what improvements will I be able to achieve in my life?

_____

_____

_____

_____

_____

JULY 11

I understand that there will be times when I find inspiration naturally and times when I will be more responsible for cultivating it through my drive and ambition. I mustn't get complacent with either one. Either way, I have a role in the outcome, so I always have a hand in it no matter what.

Is it harder for me to act on inspiration or wait for it to come? Why do I think that is? How can I bring more creativity into my profession? What would be the benefits of my enhanced creativity?

_____

_____

_____

_____

_____

JULY 12

Just like the food I eat, the content I decide to let into my mind will have an impact on me. It is important for me to take responsibility for what I view and listen to, even when it is simply entertainment. The final say is always up to me, but without taking the time to examine it, that is too big a risk to leave to chance. The health of my mind is at stake.

Regarding entertainment, how concerned am I with what I take in? Why do I have that view? What do I need to do to be more aware of the content I absorb into my mind? What can be a negative effect on my mental health from the entertainment I decide to consume?

_____

_____

_____

_____

_____

116

JULY 13

There are many different ways in which I can be happy and how I show it. It is not just about smiling and outward displays, it is about how I feel inside. My happiness can be quiet contentment in the now, or in a belief for a better future. When I do not confine myself to one definition, I am able to experience a full range of happiness instead of being disappointed with a limited version.

What are some of the different ways I experience happiness? Can I experience these freely, or do I define happiness in that singular way? What is needed for me to widen the scope of happiness I can see and experience?

_____

_____

_____

_____

_____

JULY 14

Peer pressure doesn't end after my teenage years, it just changes form. The more focused I am on how others see me, the more stock I will put into their opinions. However, when I get my worth from how I view myself, the external influences have very little power over me.

If I am honest, how much does what others think affect me? How can I begin to lessen how much I care about their opinions?

_____

_____

_____

_____

JULY 15

The more I am open to experiencing through my mind and imagination, the more I can remove the limits of the usual and common. When imagining is as much a part of the way I process the world around me, I become unburdened by the possible and extend my soul to reach my lofty dreams.

What part of my planning process involves imagination? If none, why not? If so, what role does it play and what positives have or could come from it?

_____

_____

_____

_____

_____

JULY 16

It is not realistic to expect life to never knock me down or for me to not fail. The important thing is the resilience I am able to show in the face of those missteps. As long as I understand that falling down isn't an ending, I will always have the strength to rise back up and move forward.

In what ways am I a resilient person? Recently, how have I used my resilience to grow or strengthen an area of my life? What are some results I could achieve with increased resilience?

_____

_____

_____

_____

_____

JULY 17

It is okay to have parts of my life without a specific and intended purpose; they can just exist because I like them. There is room in my life for both the necessary and the fun all at once. By seeing the value in both, I am permitting myself to include frivolity here and there.

What are some things in my life that are just there because I like them? How do I handle any feelings that say everything needs to be productive? How can I have a better handle on those feelings if they are negative?

_____

_____

_____

_____

_____

JULY 18

The most effective tool I have is awareness. When I am truly aware, I can make better, more informed choices, see where change needs to occur, and recognize the small indicators that can be easily missed in the shuffle. I will continue to work on my awareness and keep it a priority.

What role does awareness play in my decision-making? What can I do to increase my awareness regularly?

_____

_____

_____

_____

_____

119

JULY 19

Patience plays many parts in life, but the most important role is when I need to be patient with myself. It isn't always easy when mistakes occur and setbacks happen. Having the ability to be patient with my progress and the person I am despite those issues makes all the difference. The occurrences that could derail this journey of mine becomes a reminder of what is important in my life.

Am I usually patient with myself? What about when a mistake happens that is my fault? Are there ways in which I can be more patient with myself in the future? What are they?

_____

_____

_____

_____

_____

JULY 20

When I have an open mind as I go through life, I learn instead of judging, love instead of hating, and understand instead of demeaning. Having a willingness to understand others means creating a life that has a great capacity for love. The more committed I am to keeping that open mind, the more of life I will experience.

To me, what is the key to having an open mind? What could some benefits in my life be if I were more open-minded? How can I work to begin or continue bringing more openness to all parts of my life?

_____

_____

_____

_____

_____

JULY 21

No matter how much I accomplish or what I achieve, being humble enables me to find success without losing the person I truly am. The more consistent I am with making room for humility in my life, the more opportunities for success I am opening myself up to. Humility doesn't only give perspective, it lets me remember why I put in the work and effort in the first place.

Up until now, how have I worked to incorporate humility in my life? What plan do I have so that, as I succeed, I can remain humble? What does being humble mean to me?

_____

_____

_____

_____

_____

JULY 22

One way or another, everything in life comes down to perspective. What I see is not what someone else sees, but that doesn't mean someone has to be right or wrong. When I am able to understand and empathize with someone else's views, I will bring a more complete vision to my life.

When I consider a situation, do I usually see it from my perspective or multiple ones? What does that say about my method? How can I incorporate others' perspectives into my analysis and decision-making process?

_____

_____

_____

_____

_____

JULY 23

I will not let myself be confined by only what is logical and considered probable. The realistic plans I have for my future matter just as much as my dreams do. One without the other leads to an imbalance in the future. My life should consist of the freedom to reach for the goals I desire, while also respecting the realities that come with it.

What are two of my "realistic" goals, and two of my current dreams? Which ones am I working towards? Is there a way that I can work towards both my goals and my dreams simultaneously, without it being a detriment? If so, how can I begin?

_____

_____

_____

_____

JULY 24

It can seem easier for me to tell a friend what I think they want to hear, but the truth is that honesty in those intense, vital moments will be more impactful. Telling someone what they might not like is never easy, but I am going to continue working on myself so I can put their well-being first and let honesty lead me in those situations.

When dealing with friends do I tend to be honest or do I sugarcoat my opinion? Why is this my reaction? How can I be truly honest next time I am having a tough conversation with a friend?

_____

_____

_____

_____

JULY 25

While my life may not be all successes, in the moments where I did not succeed, I will strive to still find hope. It is hope that fuels my belief that I will succeed. Because life brings with it inevitable errors, without hope I cannot expect to move forward and truly accomplish what I desire.

In the past few months, what was a situation where hope played a positive role? How can I maintain hope in the future despite knowing challenges will come?

_____

_____

_____

_____

_____

JULY 26

My success relies on my ability to work and excel as it does on my willingness to rest when necessary. When I can accept rest with a positive attitude, I will be able to find refreshment even in the midst of busy times. The sooner I see rest as necessary, the easier I can incorporate it further into my routine.

What is my relationship with rest/taking it easy? How do I separate the need to rest and refresh from the stigma of seeing resting as weakness or losing time? What can I tell myself in those moments where rest is needed, but I am not willing to take a break?

_____

_____

_____

_____

JULY 27

Life is too big for me to not try new things. When I am willing to expand my horizons, I am opening myself up to not only new experiences, but new perspectives within those experiences. As I move forward, I will commit myself to being aware of those opportunities and not shying away from them when they arrive.

Here are some new things I have tried in the last few months? What are 2 things to expand my horizons that I want to try but have not yet? What is stopping me from trying them? Why are they valid reasons?

_____

_____

_____

_____

_____

JULY 28

My mind is not an inanimate object that requires no further attention. Like a plant, if I put no effort into strengthening my mind, then the opposite will happen and it will weaken. Whether they are activities, learning tools, or any other action intended to maintain my mind, the bottom line is that the worst thing I can do for my mind is assume it does not need attention.

What are some mind activities that I enjoy doing? Over the following weeks, what is a specific activity or tool that I can make a part of my routine and how will I do so?

_____

_____

_____

_____

_____

JULY 29

I must never forget that I gain nothing from an insistence on always being right. The more comfortable I get at admitting I was wrong, the more open I will be to the lessons that come afterwards. Mistakes are a part of life, but learning from them is not a guarantee. It is worth more to learn for the future than to be hard-headed for something I know isn't right.

How comfortable am I with admitting it when I am wrong? If this is an issue for me, why is that? If not, what are some lessons that stand out that I learned from admitting when I was wrong?

_____

_____

_____

_____

_____

JULY 30

By using uplifting words to describe myself, accepting compliments instead of shrugging them off, and having a positive outlook, I am building my self-esteem. I will not let the small things take away from the positive self image I am building for myself.

What do I do that positively or negatively impacts my self-esteem? What changes can I begin to make that will help in building that positive self image? What are some benefits from building my self-esteem?

_____

_____

_____

_____

It isn't only what I schedule my time for that shows my priorities, because the things that I make time for—in spite of a schedule—truly shows where I am willing to invest passion and efforts. By being aware of those situations, I can identify those areas where I put more priority, possibly without realizing it, and to make improvements where they are needed.

In the past few weeks, what impromptu things have I made time for without being asked by someone else? Why do I think those particular things took priority?

_____

_____

_____

_____

_____

Monthly Reflections

What did this last month mean to me?

_____

_____

_____

_____

What daily inspiration had the most meaning to me?

_____

_____

_____

_____

This month I learned...

_____

_____

_____

_____

Chapter Eight: August

What one person sees in their life isn't going to match up with another's view, and yet we live in a world where both can exist at the same time. The month of August is the perfect time to move forward in a spirit of understanding and acceptance, even if something seems different or you may not understand. As the Northern Hemisphere is using August to prepare for winter and wind down the hot summer temperatures, in the Southern Hemisphere they are leaving what would feel like *February*. Two very different experiences happening at the same time; no better example to use for these next 31 days.

While your hemisphere is experiencing August, what about the people around you? Those you love? This month can be a wonderful reminder to look through someone else's eyes, because when you understand someone, you can love and appreciate them in a way unique to who they are as an individual.

AUGUST 1

There will be days that are harder than others for me; that is not something I can control. What I do have control over, though, is how I choose to face it. I will be courageous in the face of a lack of desire to take action. Remaining stagnant is easy, showing courage in difficulty is not easy, but it is always worth it.

What usually causes me to just not want to start the day? What specific triggers or reasons can I begin changing right away? What benefits will being courageous have on each aspect of my life?

_____

_____

_____

_____

_____

AUGUST 2

I am only held back by the limitations I put on my mind. If I can find out my self-imposed limitations, I can work towards repairing or removing them. The more aware I become of this, the more energy I can conserve by not confining myself. I am striving to realize the power I have in my thoughts and mind, and the benefit it can bring me.

How do I limit myself in regards to what I pursue in life? What would help me believe in my mind more? How can I expand the limit of what is possible for me?

_____

_____

_____

_____

AUGUST 3

I recognize that life will not do the work for me. Opportunities will present themselves, but it is up to me to take advantage of them. I will begin taking more responsibility for the chances I do and do not take. By being more aware of the opportunities that arise, I give myself a greater chance at succeeding.

What is usually responsible for not taking an opportunity that presents itself to me? How can I strengthen my resolve in this area? What is one recent opportunity that I can begin working towards right now?

_____

_____

_____

_____

_____

AUGUST 4

I cannot promise myself that nothing bad will happen, but I can promise that I will be stronger in those times. When I stop trying to avoid the inevitable and instead prepare to weather the storm, I will grow and learn more than I ever have before.

How can I improve my reaction to life's bad times? What will help me prepare instead of worrying in the future? What are some benefits gained from taking this approach on my daily responsibilities at work or home?

_____

_____

_____

_____

_____

AUGUST 5

My awareness is not only for recognizing and identifying the negatives in life, I also need to notice the positives. There is nothing wrong with acknowledging the good things in my life. By giving attention to the joys as well as the challenges I am cultivating a more balanced, more aware way of living that will only benefit me from here on out.

Do I recognize my successes or mistakes more? Why do I think that is? How can I bring more balance to my awareness regarding the positives in my life?

_____

_____

_____

_____

_____

AUGUST 6

The best defense I have against unwise decisions and rash choices is patience. My patience can help in the long term, but I am also able to utilize that characteristic to avoid rushed situations. Sometimes all I need is a few moments to think before deciding, and being confident in my patience goes a long way to giving me those few moments.

What will help me consider patience instead of speed in those situations? What is one negative and one positive circumstance involving patience and hasty decisions? What did I learn from those?

_____

_____

_____

_____

_____

AUGUST 7

The more I am able to not only see someone else's perspective, but view their solutions as viable to my situations, the more open-minded I can be. Putting aside my personal bias and ego in order to get a more full view on the matter will never be the wrong choice to make. Being consistent in doing so will make me wiser.

What usually stops me from taking someone else's view into account? What will help me take a more open-minded approach in the future? What if I take this approach more frequently?

_____

_____

_____

_____

_____

AUGUST 8

The less reliant I am on the approval of others, the more fulfilled I will allow myself to be. Whether it is my work, creatively, or socially, I am capable of affirming myself. With an approach based on my own approval, I can have a clearer understanding of what I need and want in life.

What is one area of my life where the approval of others means more to me? Why in this area, specifically? What will start shifting the approval in that area from them to me?

_____

_____

_____

_____

_____

132

AUGUST 9

When I feel overwhelmed by life and underwater, that is when I need to have confidence in my perspective. I have power over my situation when I can pause and step back to see everything from a bigger picture view. Having perspective, especially in those moments, can make all the difference.

What can I do to be more aware in the midst of chaos and overwhelming situations? Do I feel confident in my perspective to help in those moments? If not, what needs to change?

AUGUST 10

The time I have is not infinite, so the places I choose to dedicate myself to matter a great deal. I am not obligated to give my time anywhere. By doing this, I am making my time a priority, thus giving me another chance to strengthen my self worth. If my time is a priority, then I am a priority as well.

In what ways do I not show myself that my time is a priority? How can I make the shift so that I take myself into account when considering these priorities? What would I like to do more of with the time I have?

AUGUST 11

The honesty I share with myself is only going to make an impact if I also follow through. I cannot expect honesty to work alone, because without action, it is an unfinished project. When I see what needs to be changed, thanks to my honesty, then I also need to do something about that change. The more I follow through, the more power my honesty will have.

Why have I had trouble taking action after honesty in the past? If there is a specific part of my life where this is an issue, where is it? Focusing on that area, what will help me utilize both honesty and action?

_____

_____

_____

_____

_____

AUGUST 12

Hope is like a friend who is still there when everyone else is gone. I need to take a positive approach when it comes to hope because, when everything seems to be crashing down, hope is there for me. I will not see hope as a frivolity, because it holds the real power in my life.

When was a time in my life that hope played a significant role? In what area of my life do I rely on hope the most? What am I expecting hope to help me with?

_____

_____

_____

_____

_____

AUGUST 13

All the work in the world will do me no good if I do not also see the value in rest. My goal needs to be longevity instead of simply trying to get through something. When rest becomes a regular part of my routine instead of an extra part to be crowbarred in, I will see my quality of work rise as well.

Do I tend to overdo it with work or with rest? How can I adjust those so there is a balance? What is needed to form a healthy, positive relationship with rest?

_____

_____

_____

_____

_____

AUGUST 14

The further I am willing to look outside my own life, the richer my experience will become. The assumed safety of isolation is not comparable with the vast wealth of life that is to be found in the perspectives of others. Even though it might be hard at times, I will see the power in looking beyond my horizons and value the experiences of others that I can learn from.

In my life, whose experiences outside my own have I learned from? What did I learn from them? Why was I able to open myself to their perspective and how can I use that for future situations?

_____

_____

_____

_____

AUGUST 15

The accomplishments in my life are significant to me and deserve to be recognized. When I can be affirming to myself regarding the things I achieve, I will be able to find fulfillment without the need for outside influence. While there is nothing wrong with desiring it from others, there is no replacement for being my own source of uplifting energy.

What role do others play in my affirmation? What do I need to do to be that source for my own life? What is the benefit I will achieve from being my own source of positivity?

_____

_____

_____

_____

_____

AUGUST 16

The building blocks of my life are the habits I keep. By examining the results I am getting and what I desire, I can be more aware of the kind of habits I should be forming and the ones that need to be removed or adjusted. When I make my habits a focus, I will be making a very positive step towards a balanced, healthy life in body and mind.

How much do I pay attention to the habits in my life? What are 3 habits I need to improve at home or work? What are some positive changes I can experience if I were to improve those habits?

_____

_____

_____

_____

_____

AUGUST 17

The steps I need to be taking to cultivate a positive self image should be done without judgement—from myself or others. Having good self-esteem is worth striving for, but I need to be my own biggest fan in those situations. I cannot be working towards my self image and also be fighting negativity within myself.

Would I say that my attitude helps or hurts my self-esteem? What is needed for me to create a more positive environment to grow my self-esteem? How could I be a better influence on my family if I am able to be at my optimum level of self-esteem?

_____

_____

_____

_____

_____

AUGUST 18

I will no longer allow myself to feel forced to have certain relationships in my life. The more distance I put between the people in my life and a feeling of obligation, the more sincere my relationships will be. Until I am honest and comfortable about those I choose to have in my life, I cannot be truly vulnerable with them.

Which relationships, current or past, were not beneficial to have in my life? Why do, or did I feel like they were needed? What stands in the way of me being more discerning in the future?

_____

_____

_____

_____

AUGUST 19

I may not realize it, but the belief I have in the people I love matters a great deal to them. By understanding that impact and influence I can have in another's life, I will also understand the responsibility it brings. I will respect the privilege of having a say in someone's life and strive to uplift those I love just as I would want to be uplifted.

What people in my life do I express my belief in often? What about the ones that I need to be more expressive? How would I make others feel if I were to express my belief in them? In the future, how can I be more sensitive to this and react accordingly?

AUGUST 20

The places within myself that I choose to focus on is where I will see the deepest growth. Whether it is attention to a negative trait that needs improvement, or focusing on a loving characteristic, where I invest myself is where I will excel. This is why my awareness is so important to me, because focus in general is wonderful, but when I know where to focus I will be efficiently working towards my well-being in a specific manner.

What are 3 areas of my character where I put the most focus? What about an area that I need to work on? Am I giving that attention as well? If not, what will rectify that?

AUGUST 21

I will work to be more aware of the difference between a job and a career. This is important because it will help me choose where to invest my energy. A job is short term and must be seen as temporary and a rung to something bigger and better. A career, however, is a long-term investment that will require a different level of patience and effort. Seeing the difference means I can plan and prepare wisely for my future.

Have I been investing my energy correctly regarding a career? What are my professional aspirations? What steps will help me utilize my focus better in the future?

AUGUST 22

My self-care needs to be based on the unique, individual needs that I have determined from my awareness, not based on what I want it to look like. I need to avoid the pressure to appear a certain way when it involves making unnecessary and damaging changes to my routine. Self-care is about what I need, not about optics or appearances. The deeper of an understanding I have about that, the more effective my self-care can be.

What is one aspect of my self-care routine that is not based on what I actually need? Why is it there and how can I change it? What about an aspect that needs more focus? How can I include it more?

AUGUST 23

I will not let myself reach a point where I feel like I have nothing left to learn. My life is an ever-changing, flexible journey and the more open I remain to learning, the better chance of success I give myself. By setting aside pride and ego, I will discover new depths of myself and lessons I never considered before.

In the past when I have been hesitant to learn something new, why did I have that reaction? How can I keep myself open and welcoming to new opportunities for learning?

AUGUST 24

If I am truly seeking to live a loving life, it is imperative that I incorporate empathy into every aspect of it. Empathy will help me live beyond just myself, to never assume my view is the only one, and to appreciate the experiences and views of those around me. In order to love fully and completely, I must be able to live with a consistent attitude of empathy.

Where in my life do I have struggles with being empathetic? How can I use the strong areas of empathy in my life to change those other parts for the better? What is a positive impact I can make on my friends if I were more empathic with them?

AUGUST 25

It is possible for me to live with a focused, solid work ethic and to live creatively as well. I do not need to box myself into just one thing or another. I am fully capable of finding fulfillment in both aspects of my life without having to set aside expression and creativity to find it.

Is creativity a priority for me or something extra that needs to be fit in? Why do I have this attitude? How can I make creativity more present in my life without taking away from my progress?

_____

_____

_____

_____

_____

AUGUST 26

Many problems in my life are avoidable if I learn to prepare and plan well. While I cannot avoid all of the curves in life, with focus on organization and a healthy sense of time management, I can live with a sense of preparedness instead of reactivity and anxiety.

How has my time management improved my life? What is an aspect of my time management that needs some work? What changes will help me prepare better in the future?

_____

_____

_____

_____

_____

AUGUST 27

My ambition is not something to stifle or hide. Instead, I will learn to listen to what it is telling me to plan for. When I am aware of the signals I get from my ambition, I can navigate the journey to accomplish what I set out to do. I will not let my drive be something negative, instead I will cultivate it and incorporate it into the road of life I am on.

How do I view ambition in my life? What is one direction my ambition is pointing to recently that I am having trouble listening to? Why is that, and what will help me start pursuing that?

_____

_____

_____

_____

_____

AUGUST 28

When reacting to a situation, I always have a choice; act out of impulse, or act out of rationality. I will move forward with the intent to trust my mind, despite what may be going on in my life. Choosing a positive and rational reaction will make an impact, not just on the other person, but in my life as well. The more I make that decision, the more I will feel comfortable doing so until it is natural to me.

What is a recent instance where I acted rationally despite a challenging situation? What can I learn from that to carry forward into other interactions?

_____

_____

_____

_____

_____

AUGUST 29

Even though it may seem simple, I am allowed to have things in my life just because they make me happy. I do not need to feel like I have to justify those things to myself. The more I see happiness as something of value and a need in life, the more I will make it a regular part of my efforts.

What are several things that are in my life simply because they contribute to my happiness? How can I keep myself open to my happiness in the future?

_____

_____

_____

_____

_____

AUGUST 30

The goals I want to accomplish will not just work themselves out. I will act with courage when action is needed. I recognize the work it will take, and I also acknowledge that I am fully capable of taking on what life brings with an attitude of bravery. The things that are truly meaningful to me are worth fighting for.

What was a significant time in my life when I acted with courage to reach a goal? What can I learn from that for the next situation I will need to be courageous for?

_____

_____

_____

_____

_____

<u>**AUGUST 31**</u>

The attitude with which I approach things matters a great deal. By choosing to have a positive approach I am setting the stage for productive growth to happen. I will put in the work so that I can keep negativity away from the things I am seeking to achieve. A positive environment is where true progress happens.

Do I tend to start projects with a positive outlook? If not, what do I need to do to start doing so? What growth have I seen that came from my positive approach?

Monthly Reflections

What did this last month mean to me?

_____

_____

_____

_____

_____

What daily inspiration had the most meaning to me?

_____

_____

_____

_____

This month I learned...

_____

_____

_____

_____

Chapter Nine: September

This month is a symbol for new beginnings, even later in life, or when we aren't expecting it. Autumn starts in the Northern Hemisphere while Spring is beginning in the Southern Hemisphere. Across the world, this is a chance for everything to balance itself out and prepare to move forward.

What will your beginning be this month? With all the attention given to New Year's resolutions, we often forget that fresh starts can happen at any time. What needs repairing or adjusting in your life? How will you use this to jumpstart goals you may have not thought of for some time? The possibilities are all there, it's up to you to decide which beginning will start today.

SEPTEMBER 1

The only way my dreams can be limited is when my imagination is limited as well. There is power in understanding that imagining something is the first step to making it happen. The bigger I am able to dream, the more I will be able to accomplish. I will work to avoid limiting myself and to use my imagination freely.

What is one big goal of mine that might be difficult to achieve but is worth striving for? Am I working towards it? If not, what is stopping me? And if imagining my big goal is the first step, what can I do as a second step to achieve it? What about the third step?

SEPTEMBER 2

With the right perspective and attitude, anything in my life can be an opportunity. Whether I succeed or fail, there are lessons to be learned in the experience. By putting in the effort to live with that spirit of opportunity, I will be able to learn no matter what happens.

What is a good example of a time when my positive attitude allowed me to seize an opportunity? What about when the opposite happened? What lessons can I learn from both these experiences for the future?

SEPTEMBER 3

Being truly resilient means understanding myself enough to know how to recover from a misstep. While it is important to get back up and push forward, there is also wisdom in ensuring I am ready to get back up. Putting my well-being over expediency sets a precedent for a healthy future.

What helps me bounce back after a backward step? What are some pitfalls of rushing myself that I need to avoid in the future?

SEPTEMBER 4

There is a season for everything in my life, and knowing when to move on to the next one is an important trait to have. My awareness enables me to be sensitive to the growth and possibilities in each phase of life, and when to choose the next step up.

Do I have the confidence in my awareness to trust and make a move in my life? If not, how can I enhance that awareness and confidence? What is one area, right now, where I am trusting my awareness to some degree?

SEPTEMBER 5

There is a huge difference between what I want and what I need, but both of those need to come in their own time. When I can practice self-control despite a real desire to speed up the process to get what I want, it will be because I invested time in reflection and honesty about the situation. I cannot lean one way or the other, both my wants and needs have to be approached with a different mindset about what truly matters to me.

What are 2 wants and 2 needs of mine? What is the difference between what I want and what I need? How can I better distinguish one from the other one? What is at stake if I confuse my wants with my needs?

_____

_____

_____

_____

_____

SEPTEMBER 6

I will make a real effort to react differently when I hear something I do not agree with. Instead of being impulsive or acting purely out of emotion, I will pause and try to see it from an alternate perspective than mine. I might not always end up changing my mind, but it is worth putting in the effort because when I am able to see from someone else's perspective, it will bring me growth and progress.

When I don't agree with something I hear, how do I usually respond? What could be improved about that response? How do I make my reaction come from an open-minded place? What types of things trigger my impatience?

_____

_____

_____

_____

SEPTEMBER 7

Being open to change means a willingness to accept that I might not be right. I recognize the difference between being stubborn and actually taking the time to see if I am right. As difficult as it may be at times, I will work to bring a spirit of humility to those situations.

How often do I let stubbornness take the place of discernment? How do I lessen the importance of my being right and focus on actually seeing what right is in the first place? How can I improve my decision-making skills?

_____

_____

_____

_____

_____

SEPTEMBER 8

Rather than being frustrated by things I do not know or things I have trouble learning, I will put worth in the perspectives of others to complete those gaps. Knowledge is not a one-player scenario, so the more viewpoints I welcome to my own perspective, the more varied and strong it becomes.

What are several things that I learned from others' experiences and not my own? What about recent points of frustration or distress for me? How can I start to address those points without only seeing from my own perspective?

_____

_____

_____

_____

SEPTEMBER 9

There is nothing to be gained in making myself believe something is going well. I will stop putting my short-term comfort over my long-term well-being. When I am willing to be honest with myself from the beginning, I can avoid acting from the wrong beliefs.

What is something I am going through right now that needs a more honest approach? How can I start that difficult process? What can be gained from making progress on that front?

SEPTEMBER 10

I cannot underestimate the power I have over my circumstances. The attitude and spirit I bring to each situation has a real influence on the result. By believing in hope instead of bringing a hopeless attitude, even to challenging situations, I am putting my inner power in the positive to come through.

In challenging situations, do I bring a spirit of hope or hopelessness? How can I improve or be more consistent in that reaction? How has my inner power come through for me recently? How can I enhance the strength of my inner power?

SEPTEMBER 11

A vital part about knowing myself intimately is trusting when I need to put more effort in or when I need to pause and breathe. When this decision is based on what I need instead of an external demand, I can make the best choice for myself.

Who determines rest in my life; me or another demand? How do I bring back control to myself and make better choices for my future?

_____

_____

_____

_____

_____

SEPTEMBER 12

The unknown will no longer be a place of fear for me. I am capable and strong. The unknown is indeed a place of opportunity. I will put my focus and energy in my ability to adapt and learn, so that I can take on things that used to frighten me. The power to turn the unknown into the understood lies with me and I accept the responsibility. Learning and adapting are a part of my evolution.

What are two examples of how I took on the unknown in the past? What helped me do that? What is a current unknown that I have yet to face? How can I overcome this one as well?

_____

_____

_____

_____

_____

152

SEPTEMBER 13

While I am aware of the people who mean a great deal to me and have influence in my life, that does not always mean that they are aware of it. I am determined to show recognition to those who have helped in my life. I will also work to become more comfortable in expressing that recognition in the future.

Who are three people that deserve recognition in my life? How can I do more to express that to them on a regular basis? What will start getting me comfortable with that process?

SEPTEMBER 14

My positive habits are not the only ones that should get attention. It is my responsibility to not let my negative habits slide either, even if I don't consider them a priority. Any habit that is in my life will influence who I am and what I can achieve or not. So the more attentive I am, the more improvement I can bring into my life.

What is a negative habit that I need to stop doing? How could I change it from a negative habit to a positive one? What could I achieve if I get rid of this negative habit? What does this teach me for the future about both my negative and positive habits?

SEPTEMBER 15

Having a positive self-image does not mean skewing the truth for my benefit. If I am not honest about myself, I will just be setting myself up for disappointment later on. When I am able to have an honest relationship with myself about who I truly am, I will not be influenced by what anyone thinks of me.

In what ways am I honest with myself about my self-esteem? How has dishonesty with myself harmed that? How can I avoid that in the future? What are my positive qualities I need to keep in mind for my benefit?

_____

_____

_____

_____

_____

SEPTEMBER 16

Setting a goal is the first step, but if I do not believe that I can achieve it, I am not setting myself up for success. I need to begin with a foundation of belief in myself, because only then will I be able to invest all of myself into the endeavor.

What role does self-belief play when I am setting a goal? Does it deter me from setting up my desired goals? What is an example of a way my belief in myself helped me achieve a goal?

_____

_____

_____

_____

_____

SEPTEMBER 17

I cannot succeed if my focus is only set on the long term or the short term. It will require being focused on both of those times in order for me to be truly successful. I will see both long and short term as equally important, and put forth effort in both instead of continuing to be out of balance.

Do I tend to focus on the long term or short term? How has this had an influence on my overall success? What changes do I need to make to be more balanced in this area? What are the potential benefits for me when I reach a better state of balance?

_____

_____

_____

_____

_____

SEPTEMBER 18

Being invested in my self-care means being willing to pull away when it is detrimental to my growth. This means with people, jobs, or anything that demands my attention and consumes my energy. By recognizing the positives in taking time for myself and my benefit, I will become more comfortable in making decisions based on its impact on me rather than solely on others.

What usually stops me from pulling away for self-care? What will help me see my self-care worthwhile enough to press pause for a time?

_____

_____

_____

_____

_____

SEPTEMBER 19

The freedom found in creating and expressing cannot be undervalued. I recognize that an outlet for creativity or expression in general is imperative to a healthy, well-rounded life. My creativity allows me to view and solve problems more openly and with added innovation. The details hardly end up mattering, but when I take time and focus solely on creativity, I am telling myself that I am worth this investment.

What are my preferred creative outlets? What usually gets in the way of giving them the attention I would like? What small steps can I put into practice now so that I can give them more attention?

_____

_____

_____

_____

_____

SEPTEMBER 20

Because there is no singular solution to managing my time, I will work to develop a method that works for my individual situation and priorities. By focusing on my needs instead of my wants or what others need or want, I am being true to what I actually benefit from.

What are some of my personal methods for managing time? How did I end up adding those to my life? What will ensure I remain open to further addition or adjustment?

_____

_____

_____

_____

_____

SEPTEMBER 21

It is important to understand what drives me. The more I am aware of my drive and what helps me accomplish things, the better prepared I will be for those situations. I can better navigate the journey when I understand what would assist or hinder me.

How can I determine what drives me? What are 3 things that drive me to achieve? What about 3 triggers that tend to derail progress? How can I be more aware going forward regarding both these aspects?

_____

_____

_____

_____

_____

SEPTEMBER 22

One of the best practices I can adopt is that of being selfless. When I am able to put others first I am teaching myself that it is important to focus on things outside myself. By seeing past the typical self-centered views of society, I can impact people on a very real level.

What is a recent example where I was able to practice selflessness? What can I do to keep the act of being selfless as a priority in my mind? What are the benefits of being selfless towards others?

_____

_____

_____

_____

SEPTEMBER 23

Even though I recognize that it is difficult to show positivity in hard situations, I also realize the overwhelming benefit in staying focused on the positive. When I choose to react from a positive mindset over the option requiring less effort, I am forming a habit. So the times after that, it will progressively become easier for me to choose correctly.

When did I choose positivity despite not wanting to? What did that extra effort teach me? How can I use that to make the next situation easier to handle?

SEPTEMBER 24

It is far too easy for me to pass by the wonderful things in my life and not be grateful. I will learn to move forward in a spirit of gratitude for what I am blessed with. I am willing to put in the effort so that I do not forget to be grateful when good things happen.

How can I be more expressive with my gratitude? What are 3 personal things in my life that I am grateful for? How can I show my gratitude for these things more often? What are some ways I can have more gratitude every day?

SEPTEMBER 25

I will keep myself open to discovery. The world is far too big for me to become stagnant, so I welcome the chance to discover new things. Whether it is relationships, opportunities, or just a form of enjoyment, it is worth pursuing.

What was the last discovery I made in my life? What was a positive aspect of what I learned in that moment? How can I make more room in my life for these kinds of discoveries?

SEPTEMBER 26

Life is all about chances. If I do not keep myself open to the opportunities that come around, I may not get another shot. Using my awareness, I will be able to recognize when those chances arise. Even when they don't all work out, it is worth putting the effort into the opportunity.

How has a missed chance in my past helped me to learn and become better now? How can I stay focused and aware so that I do not miss future opportunities?

SEPTEMBER 27

I am working to recognize the difference between knowledge and wisdom, but I also recognize the value in both. I need knowledge to be informed about my decisions, but wisdom is what shows me the direction that is right for me. If I only have one or the other then I will only be giving half the effort I am capable of.

To me, what is the difference between wisdom and knowledge? How does each one help my ability to make decisions? How can I build and enhance both my knowledge and wisdom?

_____

_____

_____

_____

_____

SEPTEMBER 28

The drive to succeed is not in itself a negative quality, but when it gets mixed up with my pride and ego, it can become a detriment. I understand the importance of being a driven person while also coming from a place of humility.

How can I become more ambitious? What role does my pride play in my ambition? What can I do to separate the two in future circumstances?

_____

_____

_____

_____

_____

SEPTEMBER 29

Empathy doesn't end when I know what someone thinks. It means taking the time to understand why they think that as well. The more I am able to truly see from someone else's perspective, the more depth of understanding I can have of their experience. I will also have a clearer view of what they have to offer to the world.

When was the last time I really tried to understand the "why" about someone and not just surface level? What did I gain from that experience? How can it help me be more empathetic in the future?

_____

_____

_____

_____

_____

SEPTEMBER 30

Being positive does not mean having an unrealistic view of life, it just means making the effort to look deeper. I can find the positives when I try to, it just means that I need to set aside my desire to react a certain way and instead choose to see the possibilities and believe in myself.

Do I usually associate positivity with an unrealistic perspective? If so, why? How can I change that association to a more fruitful one? How can I develop my positive thinking?

_____

_____

_____

_____

_____

Monthly Reflections

What did this last month mean to me?

_____

_____

_____

_____

What daily inspiration had the most meaning to me?

_____

_____

_____

_____

This month I learned…

_____

_____

_____

_____

Chapter Ten: October

This month can be seen as a time of transition; when the hot weather has cooled and the preparations for the colder season begins. This transitional feeling exists no matter where you are on earth. While the winter season is just around the corner in the Northern Hemisphere, in the Southern Hemisphere the preparations are for Spring to arrive instead.

No matter where you are, you can still use this month as a time to gear up for the last portion of the year. It can be stressful thinking about possible upcoming holidays, work deadlines, or school exams. While all those looming events can seem overwhelming, that is the perfect time to bring some more affirmation to your life. Building a positive attitude and developing a proactive approach towards your life will not only make excellent use of a time usually spent worrying, but when those times arrive, you will be ready and able to enjoy them.

OCTOBER 1

I have a choice between living in worry and deciding to actually deal with my worries. I will work at recognizing that just living in worry does not ease my challenges. Deciding to be prepared and to act on those challenges does put me in a better place to constructively handle those situations. Acting on what I can control is key. The time and effort ahead of time are well worth it for the result.

What are some areas of my life where I live in worry instead of dealing with the challenges I'm facing? Why do I think these specific areas are affected as they are? How can I shift my focus from the worry to the possibilities of action I am capable of carrying out?

OCTOBER 2

My life may have difficulties, but it is not set against me. When these difficulties arise, it is not wanting me to fail, it is an opportunity to learn from the experience. It won't be easy, but I can begin changing my perspective on this, so I recognize the possibilities instead of fearing the challenge. Things don't happen to me, they happen for me.

When in the past was I worried too much about something? What did I gain from worrying? Conversely, when in the past have I used difficulty to learn from it? How can I apply the same approach to my present struggles?

OCTOBER 3

The real threat to my progress isn't the unexpected things life throws at me, it is the times of inaction. When I allow stagnancy into my life it erodes my momentum and can lead to denial regarding the danger of giving in to that sense of comfort. By actively avoiding these times of being stagnant I will not miss out on progress and opportunities.

In my life, what are the differences between times of rest and being stagnant? What will help me be more aware of those differences so I can be more proactive moving forward?

_____

_____

_____

_____

_____

OCTOBER 4

I must not let myself get too focused only on how my actions impact my present self, because that action will also affect myself in the future. By not only seeing that balance, but putting effort into keeping it, I will not only be making responsible choices in the now, but ensuring it sets my future self up for success as well.

Where in my life am I responsible for negatively impacting my future by focusing too much on my present? What decisions have I taken without considering my future? What can that experience teach me about moving forward correctly?

_____

_____

_____

_____

_____

OCTOBER 5

A part of life is that things change, and what inspires me is not immune to those changes. In order for me to give myself the best chance for success, I need to be open towards those shifting drives. Just because the things that spark my ambition change throughout my life, it does not mean that the inspiration is any less than it was before.

What are two things that used to inspire me but changed as time passed? What current inspirations do I need to examine for possible changes? What is one reason I have for not adjusting those areas already?

_____

_____

_____

_____

OCTOBER 6

I will learn to stop wasting energy on only imagining what would make me happy, and begin working at making it a reality instead. The things that make me happy are worthwhile enough to not just exist in my mind. By putting in this effort, I will be proving to myself that my pursuit of happiness is important enough.

What is a specific happiness that has only lived in my mind? Why have I not tried to make it real? Are those reasons still valid today? What steps can be taken right away to put this into action in my life?

_____

_____

_____

_____

OCTOBER 7

The positive changes I want to bring to my life will not always come about easily. I need to recognize this and understand that the courage it will require doesn't mean I have to be fearless. It means that when I am afraid or worried, I can push forward in spite of it; that is what my courage can do.

When was a time in my life when courage was needed? How did I react in that situation? How can that situation help me learn when courage will be needed in the future? What might be a few things I can do to build my courage to deal with challenges at work or home?

_____

_____

_____

_____

_____

OCTOBER 8

In those times when nothing seems to be working for me, my best weapon to help me rise above the difficulty is positivity. It will not fix everything, but positivity is the first step to dealing with difficult times. I must not discount the impact that I can achieve by bringing a different, positive perspective to a situation. By keeping this in mind and close at hand, I will be ready when it is needed—even unexpectedly.

How has a negative attitude impacted events in my life? What are a few specific instances where a positive approach would have changed the outcome? What can I bring from that knowledge into my future?

_____

_____

_____

_____

OCTOBER 9

I can bridge the gap between a desire and reality by picturing what outcome I would like and how this would translate into my life. This is an important step for my preparedness, and can help focus my efforts now on what really matters. By imagining how I want it to go will influence how I navigate the situation.

Think of a desire that has been living only in my mind; if I were able to reach it, how would my life change for the better? What is the first step that I can take towards realizing my desire? And what about the second step?

_____

_____

_____

_____

_____

OCTOBER 10

My life is not defined by the times that challenge me or that even defeat me, but rather for how I responded to them. My resilience to respond is a strength that I cannot take for granted. By knowing where my strengths are and how to implement them, I can be steadfast when I am challenged.

What is one instance that stands out where I responded resiliently to a challenge? What about when my response was not correct? What was behind my actions—or inactions—in those situations? What is one thing I can learn from each situation for how I need to act in the future?

_____

_____

_____

_____

_____

OCTOBER 11

Being aware of the negatives in my life that need to be amended is productive, but it is just as important for my awareness to recognize the positive choices I make as well. The negatives can teach me, but without affirming myself for the correct actions as well, the process is incomplete and unfair to myself.

What instances or areas of my life do I have trouble affirming myself? Why does this difficulty arise? What is one of those areas of difficulty that I can work on right away?

_____

_____

_____

_____

_____

OCTOBER 12

My patience is not supposed to only extend to others, because it is just as impactful for me to be patient with myself. This will allow me to take the situations in my stride—both positive and negative. When I can be patient with myself I will give myself more opportunities to grow without judgment and to live without unnecessary stress.

How would I describe my patience level with myself? In what area am I the hardest on myself? How can I bring about changes so I can be patient with myself more than I am? What do I need to keep in mind?

_____

_____

_____

_____

_____

OCTOBER 13

Having positive self-esteem does not mean that I never feel insecure or that I am always happy with myself. It means that I am always working to improve myself and the way I see who I am. I am on a journey that requires understanding as well as my effort, both of which must be done without judgment.

What has it meant to me to have positive self-esteem? How can I improve upon those ideas so that it has less judgment and more understanding?

_____

_____

_____

_____

_____

OCTOBER 14

When I think about the values I find most important in life, that is what I should look for in the people I choose to surround myself with. There is nothing wrong with being selective about who I allow to influence me or have access to my life. The relationships I have should be built on mutual respect of values and beliefs, not tolerance of the negative traits.

For the relationships that are unhealthy in my life, why do I maintain them? Being honest, what negative impacts has my life felt from these relationships? What can I do to help me start to work through these particular relationships?

_____

_____

_____

_____

_____

OCTOBER 15

When I try to force inspiration to come, I am simply creating friction. However, when I examine my time and use patience in implementing it I will find a much more organic result. Just because inspiration doesn't come or work at one point doesn't dictate that it isn't meant to be, I just need to allow it to flow instead of forcing it.

What is something recently that I assumed didn't work because I tried to force it? Taking the time to think it over, what plan could help me try and readdress that specific instance? What are some ways in which I can spark my creativity and inspiration?

OCTOBER 16

When I find myself losing focus, the tendency to react in frustration only brings more difficulty to the situation. In those moments, the most important thing for me to remember is that patience is the tool and frustration is destructive. My focus is not served well from me getting frustrated, so by maintaining my self-control, I am giving myself a better chance to regain that focus.

What is my usual reaction when I lose focus? What are the best tools at my disposal to help with these moments? What will be a good reminder of the proper reaction in the midst of a difficult situation?

OCTOBER 17

The areas of my life that I am dedicated to may not always be lined up with what is best for me. It is important that I take the time to discern whether something is worth the time I dedicate to it. By being more particular and not just investing my energy everywhere, I will be able to give more of myself to the areas that truly matter.

Where in my life has my dedication been misplaced, either now or in the past? Why did I feel the need to invest myself in those? What is the biggest obstacle between myself and knowing where to place my dedication? How can I deal with such an obstacle?

_____

_____

_____

_____

_____

OCTOBER 18

When I am able to approach my life with complete honesty, it will allow me to see it in a much clearer way. It is through that honesty that I will be able to recognize where my energy has been wasted and where my effort should be directed towards. The more honesty I can bring to the situations in my life, the more purposeful and direct my actions will have the strength to be.

What is the biggest reason for why I have trouble being truly honest with myself? What is one area in particular where I have often had an issue with this? What will help me start to bring change to this tendency?

_____

_____

_____

_____

_____

OCTOBER 19

I am not always able to deal with trying times in my life, but I can make sure that no matter how challenging things get I don't need to lose hope. Many things may be out of my control, but I am able to hold onto the hope that things will get better. But first I must act on the things that I have control over. Without both hope and action, I am not as strong as I could be.

In the past, what has held me back from hope when difficult times happen? What am I able to do now so that in the future I will let hope play a more crucial role? How can I become better at taking action?

_____

_____

_____

_____

OCTOBER 20

I need to begin seeing the benefit and progress made not only in times of action but also in periods of reflection. It is not halting my progress, instead, it gives me a greater chance of finding insights and new angles for how to improve. Progress doesn't just mean pushing forward, it also means knowing when the most beneficial thing I can do is to reflect.

Have I tried to self-reflect on the progress—or lack of—on a recent project or task? What role could self-reflection apply to in my life? What would be the specific benefits I could achieve if I were to reflect more?

_____

_____

_____

_____

OCTOBER 21

There are moments in my life that are uniquely special to me, and because of that, I must allow myself to give them recognition. When I can freely recognize the times that stand out, I will bring more motivation to my life. Outside motivation won't always be there, but when I can build myself up, I become less reliant on others for my self-image and worth.

What are a few unique moments in my life that deserve to be recognized? How comfortable am I recognizing my accomplishments? What could help improve that for the future?

_____

_____

_____

_____

_____

OCTOBER 22

Life is full of learning opportunities, but they can easily be mistaken for roadblocks if I am not aware enough. When I respond patiently and in a discerning manner, I won't miss out when those chances come around. This will set my future up for more possibilities.

What usually prevents me from seeing learning opportunities for what they are? What is one time that I was able to recognize the chance? How can that instance teach me how to be more aware in the future?

_____

_____

_____

_____

OCTOBER 23

Creativity has many applications in my life, including being able to see and think outside the box. By seeing my creative traits as a catalyst for future positive decisions, I am giving myself a better chance to work through problems. The more I work at enhancing that creativity, the more it will be a helpful tool in my life's productivity.

What is a recent decision that required creativity for me to come to? What role would I say creativity plays in my daily life? What would help me make creativity more of a priority?

_____

_____

_____

_____

OCTOBER 24

When I do not understand something the best reaction I can have is deciding to learn more about it. The less time I spend focusing on the problem, the more energy and time I will have to formulate a solution. Information leads to more understanding, and that will help me avoid pitfalls like frustration and misplaced focus.

What is my usual reaction when I come up against something I do not understand? Has this benefited me or caused more issues? What would help me react in a more positive manner when I do not understand something in the future?

_____

_____

_____

_____

175

OCTOBER 25

There is a difference between comfort and the danger of losing momentum. I can give myself comforts without putting my productivity at risk, but I must avoid being quick to label one or the other. By being more analytical regarding this particular matter I can stop withholding comforts and still continue down a productive path.

How confident am I in my ability to tell the difference between comfort and stagnancy? What are two examples of situations that have caused me issues in the past? Looking at those from this new perspective, what is my opinion on them now? What can I learn from this for future situations?

OCTOBER 26

A key part of setting myself up for success is believing that it can happen. The confidence I have in my ability to accomplish a goal plays a huge role in the outcome. When I enter a situation with the attitude of accomplishing, plus the belief that I can do it, it goes a long way to achieving success.

How would I describe my usual attitude when setting out to accomplish a goal? Aiming for self-belief, what changes do I need to make to this approach? What is holding me back from making these changes a reality?

OCTOBER 27

It is possible for me to be at my best in both my work and personal life without sacrificing one or the other, or risking burning myself out. By widening my focus to include both career and home, I can be more aware of the balance, or lack of it. The more balanced I am able to be in the main aspects of my life, the more capable I will be of bringing my fulfillment to each.

Does my effort tend to lean towards work or home? Why do I have these priorities? Where do I need to focus on to bring balance to my life?

OCTOBER 28

While I grow from being challenged, those are not the only situations in which I can find personal growth. I need to dispel this stigma that deep growth and progress can only be found through difficulty. Life is filled with chances to grow that are not fraught with challenge, it just takes awareness and a willing perspective for me to recognize those as well as the usual rough times.

Outside of challenging times, what was a situation that helped me grow? How can this example be used to help build my awareness? What is the biggest obstacle to me noticing the difference?

OCTOBER 29

I will be more proactive in recognizing when a situation is not a good or healthy fit, and when I should press forward in confidence. This knowledge only comes through my awareness of myself and understanding what result is more beneficial to me. When I am able to recognize where my skills and talents would be wisely used and a good fit, I will find that the places I put my effort are correct.

What are my criteria to assess when a situation is a good fit or not for me; for example, a relationship with someone, or a job? When I think about what is beneficial to me, how could I stop to describe that? What are some good first steps to increasing my awareness in this area?

_____

_____

_____

_____

_____

OCTOBER 30

Because I cannot avoid the low points in life, it is important for me to know what tools help lift me out of them. By being proactive and preparing for the less than ideal times, when they do occur, I will be able to care for myself during the low moment and also have help climbing out. I can remove the stress of unfounded shame that used to come from having those difficult times with myself, and from that, I give myself the freedom to work through the experience in a healthy way.

What are some specific things that help when life gets rough? Do I usually have a healthy approach to my self-care in those times? What could serve as a helpful reminder of what helps when those times arrive?

_____

_____

_____

_____

Accomplishing a goal of mine is something significant, but the goal itself is not all that I should appreciate. I will learn more by seeing the value in the journey towards the goal just as much as the finish line itself. Without appreciating that portion of the process, I will not be as prepared for what I accomplish. A balanced approach with both areas—goal and journey—both appreciated means that I can do more with the results.

Do I usually focus on the goal or the journey along the way? What makes me lean that way? What is preventing me from having a more balanced view? How can I move forward in mutual appreciation of both portions?

<u>Monthly Reflections</u>

What did this last month mean to me?

_____

_____

_____

_____

What daily inspiration had the most meaning to me?

_____

_____

_____

_____

This month I learned...

_____

_____

_____

_____

Chapter Eleven: November

This month is unique because it is a sort of reminder that the year is coming to a close. December tends to bring finality, but November has a more calm approach, like being told you have enough time to do everything in. It is in that spirit that this month's inspirations can be drawn. So much energy and time is spent worrying about there not being enough hours in the day—and days in a month, etc.—all the while those precious minutes are ticking by.

Instead of renewing that same cycle all over again, use this month to speak productivity and completion into the days instead of anxiety and trepidation. Many cultures have attributed this particular month to the transition into the elderly years—not as an ending, but a different kind of beginning. This is yet another way of being reminded that there is more time than many believe. Even when things seem like they are winding down, there are beginnings everywhere if they can just be found.

As November starts, enter with a sense of renewal, setting aside the rush and worry that usually corresponds with this time of the year. One more inspiration as the month begins: most people don't know that the entire month is set aside for *National Gratitude Month*, so rather than waiting for one day to be thankful, take time each day to look past the negatives and find a bit of gratitude amongst it all.

NOVEMBER 1

The more I invest my energy into worrying about time, the more time I am losing. I will work to improve my mindset so that instead of focusing on how much time I have or haven't got, I will use that energy wisely. As hard as it may be to remember, time passes the same whether I focus on it or not, so worrying does nothing to improve my situation. I will focus on my most important year-end tasks and will use my time effectively and efficiently on them.

How often would I say I waste time by worrying about time? What are two possible ways I can remind myself about that in those moments? What can I do to switch my mindset from worrying into action? What resources can I access to help with this switch in my mindset?

NOVEMBER 2

There is a big difference between being productive and being constantly working or moving. Just because I am able to do something does not mean that it deserves my time and attention. When I start to see that quality matters far more than quantity, I will not only increase my productivity, but increase how satisfied I am with said progress as well.

What are several examples of things in my life that would be considered "busywork" instead of actually contributing to my productivity? Why do I give my time and attention to those kinds of things that are not deserving of it? What steps can I take to be more aware of these factors, and to hold myself accountable as well?

NOVEMBER 3

Stepping outside of a comfort zone looks different for everyone, so I can't judge my experiences by what others have done (or not done). I can be adventurous and step outside of my comfort zone while still respecting my well-being and mental stability. While one person may enjoy skydiving, another finds the same rush in completing a puzzle; my life and experiences are mine to enjoy and define.

In the last month, what is one thing I have done that was outside my comfort zone? What usually holds me back from stepping outside that zone? What is one aspect of my life where I could step outside my comfort zone? What would that bring me?

_____

_____

_____

_____

_____

NOVEMBER 4

The way I see and approach a situation will have a large impact on how I can react to it. While it may be less effort to have a negative and passive view, the positive and proactive approach is much more effective at increasing my productivity and lessening the stress it has on me. The results will reflect the change in my attitude when I combine it with my work and effort.

Do I tend to allow a situation to dictate my attitude towards it? What will help me take control of my approach to situations regardless of how challenging they are? What is one example of a time when my attitude influenced how something turned out for the good (or for the bad)? What can I learn from that?

_____

_____

_____

_____

_____

NOVEMBER 5

I will not let my friendliness or helpfulness be taken advantage of (directly or indirectly). There is nothing wrong with setting boundaries in my life, and that includes informing others when those boundaries have been crossed. The way others react to my boundaries is not my responsibility, and I cannot allow their reaction to lessen my resilience. I will get comfortable with being uncomfortable, and it is okay that I ask for space.

What is a specific trait of mine that gets, or has been, taken advantage of? Why did I let this happen? How can I be more aware in the future so that I can set boundaries and stick to them? What strategies can I implement so my boundaries are more respected?

_____

_____

_____

_____

NOVEMBER 6

Life moves very fast, and because of this it is all the more important for me to pause and express gratitude. This doesn't just mean when something momentous occurs, it is important for even the things that seem common to be recognized with gratitude. When I can be grateful and show thanks on every day, it will bring me a new depth of fulfillment and happiness for the life I have.

What kind of relationship would I say I have with consistent gratitude? Going back over the last week, what was one thing each day that I am grateful for? What will help me to be cognizant of those thankful moments throughout the day?

_____

_____

_____

_____

NOVEMBER 7

It does not take anything away from me to be kind. I do not know what others are going through in their lives, and that act of kindness might be just what they need. By keeping that positive mindset and recognizing others' experiences I will act in a way I would like others to act towards me, but without expectation.

Do I usually lean towards kindness or unkindness in moments of choice? What is my usual reason for not taking the time to show acts of kindness, and what will make me think otherwise in the future? What is one small step that I can take to show my kindness more to others?

_____

_____

_____

_____

NOVEMBER 8

Patience does not mean the need to tolerate things that are damaging to me. I will work to understand the line between what is tolerating and what is damaging so that I can maintain my patience without allowing negative results to occur because of it. When I can find the healthy limits to my patience I will be able to make smarter choices and be more aware of these limitations in the future.

Why have I let my patience become a detriment in the past? What has held me back from setting limits when it comes to my patience? In the future, how can I be patient while still pushing as hard as I can to reach my desired results?

_____

_____

_____

_____

185

NOVEMBER 9

I am a talented person, and there is no reason why I should not be proud of what I am capable of. I will stop comparing myself to others and focus on the gifts I have and what I bring to the world. When I can see my talents free from judgment and comparisons, I will truly see what I can do and what I will be able to accomplish.

What are three talents or gifts that I have? How comfortable am I with owning those gifts to others or in public? What is holding me back from truly accepting what I can do, and then showing those outside me?

_____

_____

_____

_____

NOVEMBER 10

What I do when no one is looking is almost more important than what I do in the open. The standards I have for myself should be consistent across all aspects of my life, and the more difference I allow between the private and public self, the more difficulty I will create for myself. By creating a consistent self, I will also be creating more stability and potential for my future self. What defines my character is what I do when no one is watching.

What are some differences between my public self and my private self? What are some specific negative differences that I have allowed? How can I create a balance between those two selves for the future?

_____

_____

_____

_____

NOVEMBER 11

Just like there is a season for everything, there is a time for action and effort, then a time to be more easygoing. Being more relaxed when the time allows is not a problem, it is a way of showing myself that my well-being matters and that I can achieve more results, even from unexpected places. Being able to pause and continue moving forward, but with more ease, will allow me to avoid burnout and create more opportunities for progress.

How comfortable am I with pulling back and being more relaxed? Given the chance, do I tend to overwork myself, or lean more towards being easygoing? Where is the balance needed between those two in my life? How can I bring that balance into being?

NOVEMBER 12

Learning comes in many forms, school being just one of them. There is no shame in admitting that I do not know something, but I also then need to take the next step and educate myself. The more comfortable I am with learning and finding out my blind spots consistently, the more knowledge I will allow myself to absorb. My self-education is not only important, it will lead to a better version of myself. The progress I can achieve will depend more on how I deal with not knowing than on anything I do know.

What is an area of my knowledge that I feel at ease learning about? What about an area I feel worried or anxious about that I do not know? What would help me lessen the knowledge gap and instead focus that energy on educating myself?

187

NOVEMBER 13

Understanding the differences between honesty, directness, and being overly critical of myself will be very helpful to me. The ability to speak truth and honesty without being careless with another's feelings is a valuable trait indeed. The more I am able to see from someone else's perspective, the more I will be able to give advice and speak truth into their lives without causing unnecessary damage or emotional pain.

When was a situation in which I was less than tactful with honesty? What can that teach me about being compassionate and still honest? What areas do I need to work on the most in this life lesson, and how can I start to do so?

NOVEMBER 14

My self-awareness is the key to putting my discipline into action with the most success. When I know the areas of my life that need to be focused on and the reasons to do so, I can avoid any confusion or stress. Understanding where my willpower struggles will give my self-discipline the best chance to help me work through a situation. If I am aware of my problem areas, I will be able to invest my energy wisely and find solutions with more ease.

What are a few areas of my life where I have some issues with self-discipline? Picking one, why is it a problem area for me? What will help me ignite and utilize my awareness so that I can avoid wasted energy, effort, and time in the future?

NOVEMBER 15

I am on this earth to live, not just to exist. An excellent way for me to make sure of this is to live purposefully. When I take action with purpose, I will be creating a solid foundation for my future. The more sure I am about where I want to be and how I want to get there, the more efficient my progress can be.

What does it mean to me to live purposefully? What is one area of my life where I can say I live with purpose? What about an area where I need to work on being purposeful? How can I understand my purpose for taking action?

_____

_____

_____

_____

_____

NOVEMBER 16

There is nothing inherently inadequate about being curious, as long as a sense of awareness and reasoning is brought along as well. I will allow myself the freedom to be curious, rather than resist and vilify that curiosity. This will enhance my imagination, my creativity, and give me new perspectives on life that I previously hadn't considered. Removing the negative stigma from curiosity isn't only helpful, it broadens my world.

What role does curiosity play in my life, if any? Why do I view curiosity the way I currently do, and is that viewpoint a healthy one to maintain? What can I do to make curiosity something I stop avoiding and start to see the potential positives instead?

_____

_____

_____

_____

NOVEMBER 17

Because life is always changing, the more adaptable I am, the more stress I will be able to avoid. I cannot expect difficulty or challenges to never come up, so when they occur, it is my adaptability that will allow me to not just work through them, but grow as well. The more I work at adapting, the easier it will become and the more I will start to learn from the experience.

What is my usual reaction when a situation calls for me to adapt? What improvements do I need to make to that reaction? How can I give adaptability a more prominent role in my life? How can I learn to be more adaptable to change?

NOVEMBER 18

I am not giving myself the best chance to succeed unless I can recognize needs in both myself and in others. The balance in this particular area is paramount. Only focusing on one—me or them—sets me up for a lesser fulfillment every time. When I am able to see each situation as unique, and then determine how it impacts both myself and others will give me the best chance to make well-rounded, healthy decisions.

Do I tend to focus more on myself or others? Why do I think this particular imbalance exists? How has my current perspective hurt me in the past, and then when did it help me in the past? What are some steps I can take to start leveling out this aspect of my life?

NOVEMBER 19

Productivity in the short term is an excellent goal, but I cannot forget the importance of playing the long game as well. While being productive in the short term can move things forward, when I am also bringing more long-term ideas into the mix I am focusing on my ultimate goal as well as the impact along the way. How something makes me or someone else feel can be just as important as the productivity level—both in the long and short term.

What differences do I see between being focused on being productive in the short term compared to the long game? What is one example of a time when I was only seeing the short term when I should have included the element of the longer game as well? How can I use that experience to be more aware of the importance of being productive in both the long and short term?

_____

_____

_____

_____

_____

NOVEMBER 20

I am worthwhile, and because of this, the goals and dreams I have are valuable as well. Having this perspective will let me be ambitious without attaching any guilt or limitations to it. By viewing myself as someone worthy of success and happiness, I am giving myself permission to not just recognize my ambitions, but to pursue them as well. The things I want and aim for are important simply because they are mine.

What are two ambitions of mine that I have not felt comfortable being open about? Why do I feel this way about those ambitions? What would give me more freedom to express one or both of those?

_____

_____

_____

_____

NOVEMBER 21

Enthusiasm can mean different things to each person, while still maintaining its impact. I do not need to match anyone else's enthusiasm to show my own life and goals the support they deserve. When I remove the judgment from that picture, I will start to see a more open approach to the kind of enthusiasm I bring to life.

What are some ways that I express my enthusiasm? What issues have I dealt with regarding how others' enthusiasm has impacted how I show mine? What will help me be more focused on myself for future situations?

_____

_____

_____

_____

_____

NOVEMBER 22

It is not my responsibility to make others feel comfortable when it takes precedence over my feelings. Life is full of good days and bad days, and I can experience both in the ways that fit my life. How someone else reacts to my feelings is theirs to deal with, and I will work at accepting that as a truth in my life. I am allowed to feel the way I feel.

In the past, why did I let others impact the way I expressed my feelings? What have I learned from that since? What has been a common reason for me letting someone else's feelings take precedence over mine? How will I work to change that reason?

_____

_____

_____

_____

_____

NOVEMBER 23

I do not need to fabricate positive emotions in order for me to classify a day as "good". I can have different standards for each day, even when it means going easy on myself for the sake of my well-being. I am taking stress away from myself by also removing the need to classify the day; I can be happy without needing to qualify it.

What usually qualifies as a good or bad day to me? Why do I feel the need to classify my days as one or the other? What do I think will help me remove that need in the future?

NOVEMBER 24

There is room for me to be both trusting and cautious at the same time. Just like in the rest of my life, it comes down to balance. It is important to be trusting and vulnerable, but I recognize the importance of being wary about who or what situation gets that part of myself. By balancing both trust and caution, I can experience the fullness of life while still seeing my well-being and stability as a priority.

Do I find it more natural for me to be trusting or cautious? What is one way this perspective has hurt me, and one way it has helped me to grow? What is one step that will help me be more balanced between my trust and the caution I bring to life?

NOVEMBER 25

Just because something has been done before does not mean it isn't worthy of being appreciated. Regular appreciation—of both myself and others—will give me a more grateful perspective for life as a whole. By prioritizing appreciation over expectation as an important part of me, I am giving it the chance to have a positive impact on both myself and those in my life.

Do I regularly show appreciation? Why or why not? How has appreciation positively impacted me in the past? What would help me keep appreciation in mind for future situations? What can I appreciate about my life today?

_____

_____

_____

_____

NOVEMBER 26

By truly listening to others, I will learn the benefit of patience and prioritizing others over myself. Knowing the difference between talking to people and listening to them is taking a real interest in what they say instead of waiting for my turn to speak. When I can make this kind of listening a regular part of who I am, I will see increases to my personal growth as well.

Do I tend to listen to others or simply talk with them? What can help me listen more? What steps can I take so that I am consistent in this and not just listen sporadically?

_____

_____

_____

_____

NOVEMBER 27

While there is nothing wrong with me expressing my emotions, there is value found in maintaining my temperance, especially in situations that rarely result in it. Because I know that life's challenges cannot be fully avoided, when they do occur, I can maintain control of the situation by not losing my composure. When I react in a stoic manner, I will find more and more that the challenging situations become manageable and solutions are more readily available. Temperance is a habit that can be developed.

What is a situation where I usually have trouble keeping my composure? Why is this? What would help me maintain that control for when that situation occurs in the future?

_____

_____

_____

_____

_____

NOVEMBER 28

If I choose to focus solely on the results of my endeavors, then I will be controlled by the outcome. However, if I decide to focus on the process rather than the outcome, I am able to take back control. There will be times when things do not go the way I would have liked, but by focusing on where my attention and energy go, I will be sharpening my discipline and focus towards the end-goal. My appreciation can determine the way I end up seeing an experience, so aiming it towards positive growth will give me the opportunity to find good among the bad.

What are some situations in which I find it hard to focus more on the process than on the outcome? Why does this difficulty exist? How can I make my renewed focus on the process more of a priority than the result of a situation?

_____

_____

_____

_____

NOVEMBER 29

My awareness doesn't only give me the best chance to make positive choices, it also allows me to be more specific in expressing myself. When I know why something bothers me, or why I enjoy something, I can express it better to both myself and others. This allows me to be a better friend, partner, and family member because I can tell others both what I am feeling and how best to help me. Every chance to increase my awareness is always time well spent.

What is one area of my life where I feel comfortable expressing myself, and one in which I find it difficult? What tends to create difficulty when I try to express myself? What is one recent situation where I overcame the challenge and was able to express myself? How can I get better at that?

_____

_____

_____

_____

_____

NOVEMBER 30

My ability to manage my time truly comes down to how honest I am willing to be with myself. When I can allow that self-honesty to dictate how I prioritize my time, I will be able to do so without the worry that I am overwhelming myself or not doing enough. When my time-management is based on what is actually the best for me, I can be the best for both myself and others.

What is one example of how my time-management has prioritized others over myself? What is an example of the opposite, when I prioritized based on what was best for me? What will help me use the best time-management for my interests in the future?

_____

_____

_____

_____

_____

Monthly Reflections

What did this last month mean to me?

_____

_____

_____

_____

_____

What daily inspiration had the most meaning to me?

_____

_____

_____

_____

This month I learned...

_____

_____

_____

_____

Chapter Twelve: December

January generally holds the air of a fresh start and renewal after a long year, but you can only discover that renewal after you have reflected over the events of the 300 days that have come before. That is where December comes in—because reflection is right in its wheelhouse.

No matter where on the globe you are—snow or warmer weather—the end of the year tends to bring a plethora of emotions into play and that can be a lot to handle at times. It can be far too easy for a period of peaceful reflection to become a stress-filled month instead. Rather than just anticipating the challenges and "pushing through", this is the chance to take back control of a time of year that can set the tone for the next phase of life.

This doesn't need to be a countdown, which it tends to be framed as, because again that puts way too much stress on an already strained time. Think of this as a great warm-up that will lead to a better, more productive coming year. Thirty-one more chances to inspire and build on the foundation that *you* have created and strengthened—not a bad way to write a close to what will just be one of many chapters in your life.

DECEMBER 1

My word should mean something; not just to others, but to myself as well. When I am sincere and transparent, it will display my true integrity. Investing my effort and focus on building my character is always a worthwhile use of my time.

What role does sincerity play in my life? In what areas could I work on improving my sincerity? Why do I struggle in those specific areas? How could I start improving my character?

_____

_____

_____

_____

DECEMBER 2

There are many aspects of my life that should be handled in a serious manner, but I cannot forget the importance of including humor. Whether it is in times of stress or difficulty, alleviating the intensity can work in my favor. When I see humor as a tool in my life rather than a luxury, I can improve my relationship with it and learn what role it plays for me.

How would I describe my sense of humor? Do I welcome humor in my life, or does it "get in the way"? What can I do to help me learn about my humor, and how it can be implemented in my life?

_____

_____

_____

_____

DECEMBER 3

As stressful as my life can be, I need to remember that others are experiencing their own struggles as well. It does not take away from me when I show kindness and friendliness to another person. By recognizing that I can have a positive impact on someone else, I will be working on expanding my worldview and to see outside my own perspective.

When was the last time I was friendly towards someone despite the struggles in my own life? How did that help me grow as a person? What can I do to be consistent in my friendliness despite what is going on with me?

_____

_____

_____

_____

_____

DECEMBER 4

There is value in being a reliable person. By doing so, I am showing respect to others and their time, but I am also giving myself the opportunity to have other qualities to shine within me. By making the effort to be more reliable to others and myself, I will enhance both personal and professional relationships.

How reliable of a person would I say I am? What is one positive and negative instance where my reliability was present and then not? What are a few steps I could take to make reliability a firm priority to me?

_____

_____

_____

_____

_____

200

DECEMBER 5

When I am able to do things in the present that will benefit my future self, I will begin to live and act in more than just the "now". By prioritizing the future version of who I am, it helps me to consider the quality of the decisions I make now and how they will impact me down the road. This will help me with my patience and in how I prioritize in my life overall.

How would I describe the future version of myself I am striving for? What is an example of a recent time I acted with my future self in mind? How did that benefit me in both the present and later on? What is the biggest roadblock between who I am now and the ideal future version of myself?

DECEMBER 6

When it comes to my productivity, stress is one of the biggest enemies of my forward progress. Because stress tends to manifest itself as distraction, when I am aware and prepared for the distractions, I will be giving my productivity the chance to succeed. The less stressed and less distracted I am, the more progress I will be able to make and the more productive my work will be.

What are a few of the more common distractions that get in the way of my productivity? What are some steps I can take to start regaining control over my productivity? What is an example of a consequence in my life that could come from the distractions winning out?

DECEMBER 7

Life's challenges will never cease completely, so it is all the more important for me to be able to maintain a calm demeanor when those challenges arise. Challenges are not a negative in life, rather they are what allows me to grow, to gain experience, and to become a better version of myself. Rather than denial, I will be prepared and have a realistic approach when life's challenges occur. By keeping calm in those situations, I will be able to learn and grow from that challenge.

What is my usual reaction to the more stressful times in life? What will help me prepare and plan ahead? In the past, what is the reason I usually lose control? What can this teach me about staying calm in the future?

DECEMBER 8

Kindness is one of the most important and overlooked traits I can have, but not just towards others, towards myself as well. The way I treat and speak about myself has an impact on the self-image I maintain, so the kinder I can be, the more healthy that image can be. I am able to treat myself with kindness and still have a realistic view of life. By giving myself the freedom to change I am proving my worth to myself, and showing that I care about the person I am and who I am becoming.

Is the way I think about and speak about myself usually positive or negative? Why do I have those negative views of myself? What usually hinders me from treating myself kindly? What developments of self-care are needed for me to treat myself with more kindness? What can I do to treat myself more kindly?

DECEMBER 9

While it may be easier to slide into the negative habits I have, by investing my energy and focus on the positive habits in my life I will be giving priority to the healthier, happier side of myself. The negative habits deserve focus to be worked on, but too often the positives get lost in the mix. I am capable of seeing both types of habits, but I have control over how I approach each.

What are three positive habits I have? Was it easy or difficult to think of those positive habits? What tends to make my focus lean towards the negative, and how can I begin to bring change there?

DECEMBER 10

Instead of struggling to create a work-life balance, I will start to strive for harmony. This means that I will not be controlled or overly influenced by the emotional roller coasters that come from trying to fully exist in both places. Harmony is about boundaries rather than struggling and stressing over balance.

What area of my life do I tend to struggle with the boundaries of harmony? Why do I struggle in that particular area? What is standing between me and finding harmony amongst the different areas of my life?

DECEMBER 11

There is a huge benefit to being able to know how and what I need for my own self-care. I cannot ever see my awareness as anything but a positive, because it is through that awareness I can learn what truly refreshes and helps me reset. Because I know and accept that life will bring difficulties, knowing ahead of time what will allow me to maintain my path and pace through self-care and fortitude, I will be able to establish a positive mindset that will translate to good feelings and emotions for others around me.

What are two specific types of self-care that are the most effective for me? What usually stops me from putting those into action when needed? In the future, what will be a reminder that taking time to focus on self-care is not "giving up" or anything of the sort?

_____

_____

_____

_____

_____

DECEMBER 12

Creativity comes in a wide variety of forms, and because of this, it is important for me to explore where mine is. By discovering the details of my creativity, I will be able to channel life's stresses and challenges into something positive and productive. I will be accepting of my personal kind of creativity, and respect it as a vital piece of my well-being and stability.

What are a few specific types of creativity that I consider unique to me? What tends to hold me back from exploring those areas when needed? How do these creativities add positivity and joy to my life? How can my creativity help me with other aspects of my personal and professional life?

_____

_____

_____

_____

DECEMBER 13

By recognizing the benefits of keeping a regular journal, I am giving myself another tool of self-reflection to help me not only improve myself, but understand myself better as well. This will give me a healthy outlet that I can rely on to be a safe space to vent and explore my thoughts. The effort spent in finding the journaling method that works for me is well worth the benefits that will come from it in the future.

In the past, what has been a reason that I struggled to keep a journal or a similar method of self-reflection? What can I do so that this time it becomes a positive habit? What are a few small steps that I can start now to help include journaling in my daily life?

_____

_____

_____

_____

_____

DECEMBER 14

I need to be aware of my own negative tendencies so that I can avoid self-sabotaging. By being transparent with myself and addressing my struggles, I will end the destructive cycle of being ashamed and instead be able to focus on finding healthy outlets. The way I treat and speak about myself matters, so by acting in a positive way towards myself, I will stop self-sabotage before it can take root.

What is a kind of self-sabotage that has been an issue in the past for me? What can I do this time so I avoid self-sabotage and instead build myself up? What are some daily ideas that can help me maintain that healthy perspective?

_____

_____

_____

_____

_____

DECEMBER 15

My life is not determined by the troubles and struggles I have gone through, but rather in the responses I have had towards them. By recognizing that resilience is not a permanent state, but a way of growth, I can see my experiences through a more positive lens, and as a result, I can take some constructive steps to help myself. I am not defined by the negatives, because every life has them, but by my responses. Because with every situation and challenge I face, I prove to myself that I have the freedom to choose my reaction.

What is one specific instance where I showed the definition of my resilience? Do I usually give myself credit for what I have endured and gotten through? Why or why not? How can I see myself as that resilient person in a positive light for the future?

_____

_____

_____

_____

_____

DECEMBER 16

It is absolutely worthwhile to be patient with others, but a commonly forgotten aspect of this is also being patient with myself. Whether this means reviewing my standards or being more understanding about what I have gone through, I deserve to show myself patience. When I see my life through that view of patience, I will be able to avoid being hard on myself when it is unnecessary and unproductive.

Am I usually patient with myself? When I am not, why do I usually not have that patience? Do I find it easier to be patient with others than myself? Why is that? What can that teach me for how I react towards myself in the future?

_____

_____

_____

_____

_____

DECEMBER 17

The more honest I am with myself, the more growth I will have the chance to obtain. There is no long-term benefit found in being dishonest with myself. All it does is create a divide between what is reality and how I see things. It may not be easy, but the more consistent I am with my self-honesty, the more problem areas I will be able to recognize and start to repair.

What specific areas of my life do I tend to avoid being honest with myself about? Why those areas? What is the reason I have for not being completely honest with myself? What are the first few steps I can take to see this as worthwhile and make it a priority?

DECEMBER 18

The experiences that I have gone through in life are an incredibly valuable source of wisdom for my future, if I reflect on them. Whether the situation worked out well or not, by acting in awareness, self-reflection, and transparency, I can look back and gain wisdom for the experiences that have yet to happen. When I can understand this and believe in the wisdom gained, I will have more help in the future.

Answering honestly, do I see my experiences as giving me wisdom? If not, why? What is one example of an experience that taught me a lesson I was able to use in a future, similar situation? What does this tell me about the process of self-reflection?

DECEMBER 19

The way I react when someone else does something that does not work out will give a glimpse into how understanding of a person I am being at that moment. By seeing another's actions as though they were mine, I can bring more empathy into the situation. When I am able to temper my reaction and instead see it from another viewpoint, I can avoid a negative, swift response and instead act with understanding and kindness.

In the past, when I have not acted with understanding and/or kindness towards someone else, what was usually the reason? What can I learn from that so I can apply it to future situations? How can I make empathy a more regular occurrence, even when the interaction isn't necessarily a positive one?

DECEMBER 20

When I give my full effort and attention to something, I have the ability to experience a flow state of mind that enhances my focus and abilities. The effort and time that I invest in getting to that flow state is worthwhile because from there my productivity and progress can reach new heights. By giving myself the chance to reach flow state I am showing myself another way in which I prioritize myself and my productivity.

What would be some examples of roadblocks between myself and my flow state? What are some ways I can reach my flow state faster and more efficiently? What will help my preparedness so that I can avoid distractions and focus on my productivity?

DECEMBER 21

The true test of my willpower and discipline occurs when there is no immediate consequence other than my own view. By first recognizing a situation as significant, I can prepare and invest my energy in being self-disciplined. The more consistent I am in this, the stronger my willpower will become and the more confident I will be in my ability to be self-disciplined even when I am alone. To strengthen my willpower, I will begin recognizing the reasons for the decisions I make or fail to make. Any behavior that I am unaware of is much harder to manage.

What is one area that consistently tests my self-discipline? What efforts have I made in the past to help this? What growth has been made? Learning from this for the future, what can I begin to do so that when my willpower is tested, I can respond well?

_____

_____

_____

_____

_____

DECEMBER 22

I am not perfect, and because of this, it means I have made mistakes in life and in the future I will not always make the correct choice. Knowing and accepting this, it is vital that I can show myself forgiveness for the times I did not choose wisely. I can hold myself accountable and learn from the mistakes, but the most important part of the process is being able to forgive myself. This may not be easy or quick, which is okay, because daily attention to this part of myself will end up being invaluable for a healthy, positive future.

What areas in my life do I struggle with forgiving myself? Why is it difficult for me to do so in those areas—in general as well? What changes will help me include forgiveness in the way I view and take action for my self-care?

_____

_____

_____

_____

DECEMBER 23

When I am able to accept and love my unique self, it will allow me the freedom to appreciate the originality that comes with it. Being different is rarely easy, but by truly seeing and understanding the person I am, I am showing the original part of me that it is welcomed, appreciated, and accepted.

What are a few aspects of myself that I consider original or unique? What kind of relationship do I have with those aspects? What would allow me to be more accepting of the originality that exists in my life? How can I leverage my originality or uniqueness to progress in life?

_____

_____

_____

_____

DECEMBER 24

My awareness does not exist to help me recognize only the positive things in life, it becomes truly priceless when it alerts me to the negatives. Seeing the positive parts is important without a doubt, but it is only half the process without also seeing the negatives. I understand that both exist within me and in my life, so when I am aware of both the positives and negatives, I can respond well. I do this by accepting and taking joy in the positive, but also in exploring how to improve and repair the negatives.

Through my awareness, do I tend to focus on the positives or negatives? How has this both helped and hurt me in the past? What would I consider a couple of my negatives? And how could I improve them?

_____

_____

_____

_____

DECEMBER 25

It takes confidence to overcome many things in life, but humility is what allows me to see past my pride and ego down to the truth. Even with excellent awareness, my mind can sugarcoat the issues, which avoids the difficulty of seeing it but also removes the chance to bring change. When I can set aside what I want and aim for what I need, I will be able to strengthen my humility as well as my view of reality.

What relationship do I have with humility? What issues do I tend to have when trying to act from a humble place? When was a time that humility allowed me to see something I would have missed otherwise?

_____

_____

_____

_____

DECEMBER 26

It can be very easy to see all the difficulties, negatives, and issues that may arise in the future, but unless it is also tempered with hope, it will only bring me stress. It is important to be prepared for what will come as long as there is no despair involved. Hope is not setting myself up for disappointment, it gives me the freedom to believe that I can succeed and accomplish what I set out to do.

As of right now, what are a few things that I am hopeful for? How has hope been a positive in my life? What must I do to maintain hope and to keep negativity at a distance?

_____

_____

_____

_____

DECEMBER 27

In the bustle and complexities of life it can be far too easy to have things slip my mind. This is why it is so important for me to remember the relationships in my life that are worth investing my time and energy into. Healthy, long-term relationships of any kind require effort and consistency. By recognizing the areas that I struggle in maintaining those relationships I can be more aware in the future and avoid causing damage to them.

What in my life usually causes relationships to slip my mind? What could be a few useful reminders when those tendencies occur? In the past, what is one example of a time when I recognized that moment and was able to avoid damaging the relationship? What can that teach me for the future?

_____

_____

_____

_____

_____

DECEMBER 28

Life may have mistakes, but it is important to not label those as failures in my eyes. Instead, I need to see each of those results as another chance to learn something about myself and life. Making the shift from a negative perspective—failure—to the positive one that is a learning opportunity will lead to more growth, more chances to learn, and have long-term benefits overall.

How can I begin to see the more challenging areas of life as chances to learn instead of seeing them as failures? Why do I struggle in those areas? What changes could I put into action so that I can make the switch from failure to learning?

_____

_____

_____

_____

DECEMBER 29

I cannot let the pace of life dictate the speed at which I make decisions. When I give up that control, I lose the chance to prepare or to take time to consider the situation. The pressure from life's many stressful areas can make it incredibly hard to choose my speed over life's but in the end it will result in better choices and more productivity. The more it happens, the more confident I will become in choosing preparation over speed.

What areas of my life cause the most pressure regarding speed and pace of choices? How do I usually respond in those situations? What would help me to be steadfast despite the pressure and prioritize my pace instead?

_____

_____

_____

_____

_____

DECEMBER 30

I do not have an endless supply of emotional energy. By recognizing my limits, I will be more cognizant of where I invest that energy throughout the day. The more aware I am of this, the more I will be able to regulate the areas that deserve my energy and those that do not. Taking back control of my energy investment doesn't only increase how productive I can be, it also proves my worth to myself as I am my own priority.

What are two areas that deserve to have my emotional energy, and two that I tend to invest in that should not be? Why were those two areas not worth my energy investment? How can that help me make similar, positive recognitions in the future?

_____

_____

_____

_____

_____

DECEMBER 31

Being able to recognize myself for the things I accomplish is a very worthwhile practice to keep. I put effort and energy into the things I work towards, and because of this, I recognize that there is nothing wrong with celebrating myself. I began a journey one year ago and the fact that I am here now is something certainly worthy of recognizing. I will continue in that spirit and remember that I am valuable and the dedication I put into my goals is worthwhile as well!

What are several things in the past year that I am particularly proud of? Did I recognize those accomplishments in the moment? If not, what will help me maintain a spirit of recognition and self-appreciation in the future? What message for myself would I like to leave here for my future self to come back to?

_____

_____

_____

_____

_____

Monthly Reflections

What did this last month mean to me?

_____

_____

_____

_____

What daily inspiration had the most meaning to me?

_____

_____

_____

_____

This month I learned...

_____

_____

_____

_____

Conclusion

As we all go through life and time passes by it can be very easy for all our focus to be on the time that it feels like we're losing. The more attention that we pay to how fast it's passing, the more chunks of life speed right by. It isn't just the time in terms of hours, days or weeks, it is time spent without reflecting on our lives. Time without any form of self-improvement.

What we have done over this past year, though, has been remarkable because it was so much more than just reading words every day; we took back control and got to know ourselves better and deeper than before.

We may feel at times that we have no control over the things that affect and direct us, but one thing we do have control over is our minds and souls. We have the power to redirect our bodies to more constructive ways of viewing life, to believe in our ability to rise above the obstacles placed in our way and to have the confidence to do more than just exist and make it through the day. What we have done for the last year is not only to grow but to discover areas to improve upon that we hadn't even noticed before.

Now, there is good news and better news. The good news is that this wasn't just a replacement for a journal or something to do in the morning, this was the key to getting back to our foundation and strengthening it through confidence, self-awareness, and most important, action.

What about the better news? The better news is that this journal is intended for use year after year. It isn't like a calendar that can be discarded on the 31st of December. We can start another journal whenever our new year begins and continue on our pathway to self-improvement.

Use the completed journal to reflect on how things have changed since those notes were made, especially those written in the early days. How far did you go on your journey? Did you reach your goals or did you fall short in certain areas? Consider the inspirations that gave you the drive when exhaustion was winning, the lessons that helped you learn what was truly important, and the habits that were negative and are now positive and productive, which is quite the double feature!

The point is that we have accomplished something that may not have started out as a life-changing journey, but look where we are now! We should take a moment and recognize the changes we have made in ourselves and to our lives in general over the past year. It's not an ending, either, not even close! This is the beginning of a new chapter in our lives, one written in the spirit of responsibility, ownership, ambition, and renewal. Each page holds a new and exciting opportunity to expand our horizons and develop parts of ourselves that have gone without attention for far too long.

We did this! We made this all happen! It wasn't magic or an illusion—we changed our reality and we can continue that positive change every single day moving forward. There is no need for me to give you advice about being diligent when it comes to these positive steps, because the kind of deep, lasting improvements of self that you have followed through on don't just have a surface-level impact, they make changes down to the core.

What will this new you accomplish in the next year? What adventures await as the next journey unfolds before you? The only option is to do exactly what you did to get to this point—take the first step because *this is your way*!

THANK YOU!

Thank you very much for giving me the opportunity to contribute something positive to your life. I hope this book will help you, and that you will enjoy what you can achieve after reading the positive affirmations and writing your responses to the powerful questions. I also hope that this book makes you reflect and that it fills you physically, psychologically, and spiritually. Thank you again!

Please, I want to ask you a small favor.

I do not have a large company, nor do I have a publishing company helping with the marketing and promotion of this book. I wrote and produced this book on my own. As a result, I will be very grateful if you can please give me a review on Amazon.

With your review, this book can improve (or worsen) its ranking on Amazon and become more visible to others, so that they can too benefit from it! **To give me your review on Amazon, please scan this QR code**.

Thank you very much in advance for your support!

Mauricio

Made in the USA
Monee, IL
21 December 2022

23207116R00132